SECRETS
OF SUPER
ACHIEVERS

PHILIP BAKER

WHITAKER
HOUSE

deepercalling

SECRETS OF SUPER ACHIEVERS
ISBN-13: 978-0-88368-806-9
ISBN-10: 0-88368-806-9
Printed in the United States of America
Australia: © 2004 by Philip Leonard Baker
United States of America: © 2005 by Philip Leonard Baker

WHITAKER
HOUSE

1030 Hunt Valley Circle
New Kensington, PA 15068
www.whitakerhouse.com

deepercalling.com

Library of Congress Cataloging-in-Publication Data
Baker, Philip (Philip Leonard)
Secrets of super achievers / Philip Baker.
p.   cm.
Summary: "Looks at the characteristics that make up a super achiever,
encouraging readers to pursue excellence in character, leadership, and faith"—
Provided by publisher.
Includes bibliographical references.
ISBN-13: 978-0-88368-806-9 (hardcover : alk. paper)
ISBN-10: 0-88368-806-9 (hardcover : alk. paper)
1. Success. I. Title.
BJ1611.2.B33 2005
158.1—dc22   2004028279

1 2 3 4 5 6 7 8 9 10 11 **ш** 12 11 10 09 08 07 06 05

Contents

Acknowledgments 7

Preface 9
Why Equality Is Not for Us

1. The Quest for Character 15
   Inward and Onward

2. Just a Puppet on a String 29
   Responsibility

3. Daze of Our Lives 37
   Overriding Goal or Passion

4. You Have to Jump in the Puddles 49
   Optimism

5. Fatal Distraction 61
   Focus

6. It's Not Checkout Time Yet 71
   Endurance

7. In Praise of Super Achievers 87
   Abundance Mentality

8. My Brain Hurts 97
   Constant Learning

9. Lifestyles of the Rich and Miserable 109
   Contentment

10. Flying with the Ducks 121
    People Believers

11. Keeping out of the Ditches................................129
     Balance

12. First You Have to Get out of Bed.............................137
     Discipline

13. I'm Bigger on the Inside................................149
     Self-Growth

14. The Upside of Down 157
     Humility

15. Fortune Favors the Brave................................169
     Courage

Epilogue 177
     Further on, Further in

Endnotes 183

About the Author................................187

Acknowledgments

I would like to thank:

My wife, Heather, for her love and the incentive plan.

Penny Webb for her encouragement and confidence in me. It was her hard work that converted the ideas of this book into what you hold in your hand.

Wes Beavis, who kept telling me to write a book and was most helpful in scrutinizing the text before it was published.

The many friends, students, and coworkers who read and reread the early drafts of this book—Mark Webb, Mark Pomery, Christine Reeves, Bree Elliott, Jillian MacLachlan, Moira McLean, Pat Mesiti, Graham Irvine, Pam Howie, and Rosemary Crooks.

All those who call Riverview Church their home. The great privilege of leading a church, and the thinking and speaking such a position entails, gave me the place and the reason to communicate things that really matter.

Preface
WHY EQUALITY IS NOT FOR US

"Great men are little men expanded; great lives are ordinary lives intensified."

Wilfred A. Peterson

Preface

I believe that every human being has been created with greatness in mind. Within us all is a deep well of incredible potential. As Bob Richards, the Olympic pole-vaulter, said, *"There is genius in every person."* Zig Ziglar's favorite expression runs along similar lines: *"People are designed for accomplishment, engineered for success, and endowed with the seeds of greatness."* While I believe these sentiments with all my heart, I realize that not all people reach their potential. Indeed, very few could die totally satisfied with the fact that they did everything, and were everything, they could have been.

I have spent most of my life thinking and speaking about potential and the desire for success. How can I be all that I can be? How can I help others realize their potential? One of the tragedies of life is that many of us settle for just getting by rather than reaching for success. We have developed a maintenance mentality that minimizes the pain in life but does not allow us to strive for mastery. But at the same time we look up to those who excel and call them lucky or blessed. We want to be like them, and we often try to imitate their behavior and learn from their lives.

It is easy with such an undertaking to focus on the wrong thing—to try to copy the actions, skills, and practices of the successful rather than getting to the heart, the inner working, of such a life.

Most of us want to be who we were designed to be and live a life of excellence. Over time, we learn that what is within us is the principal thing. We begin to draw water from the reservoirs of our souls and come to the realization that our futures are flexible. We can set our own level in life. This understanding alone causes us to raise our expectations and, as a result, to rise and live abundant lives.

Unfortunately, others respond more negatively to the successful individual. These people's hearts are filled with envy, secretly delighting in the failure of others and critical of any who are achieving beyond the norm. Such smallness of spirit is the seedbed for town gossip and harmful attitudes toward the very leaders who could help us rise to their level. In examining this human phenomenon and its impact upon the economics of community and nations, George Gilder gives an illustration from the work of Edward Banfield, *The Moral Basis of a Backward Society.*

> *In the small town in Italy that he studied in an effort to understand the sources of poverty, every businessman was assumed to be cheating his employees, every priest to be filching from the plate, every politician and police-man to be on the take. A teacher justified his laziness by confiding that the only use of education was to better exploit the poor. Any signs of prosperity were taken as evidence of peculation or crime. Needless to say, in such a town few such signs appeared.[1]*

Such people's basic philosophy is that, despite effort and initiative, we are all meant to be the same and have the same in life. Anything else is either evidence of wrongdoing or simply unfair.

Personally, I believe that life is not and cannot be this way. Things such as wisdom, hard work, and the willingness to go the extra mile actually do make a difference. Life is not a zero-sum game. Egalitarianism, which thinks nothing of punishing achievement and rewarding inactivity and laziness, must be quashed from our consciousness if we are to rise to new levels in life.

Yes, we have incredible potential, but we will only achieve in life when we begin to stretch ourselves and realize that a life of abundance will not suddenly appear just because we are good people. We need to do things, believe things, and think in new ways. This book is all about becoming a Super Achiever in life. It is written to the person who desires to plumb the depths of his or her own being and then grow; to the person not satisfied to simply be; to those who want to move beyond mediocrity and push themselves to excel.

THE QUEST FOR CHARACTER

Inward and Onward

"No man can tell whether he is rich or poor by turning to his ledger. It is the heart that makes a man rich. He is rich according to what he is, not according to what he has."

Henry Ward Beecher

Chapter One

The Quest for Character

Our character is what we do when we think no one is looking. —Karl Otto von Schonhausen Bismark

I recently experienced the truth of the above quotation in an embarrassing way. I was visiting Ripley's Believe It or Not! Museum in San Francisco. Following the walkway that led through a maze of the strange, the remarkable, and the bizarre, I came to a series of booths that each contained a mirror, as well as a description of how some people are specially gifted to contort their faces in unusual ways.

"One in 10,000 can touch their nose with their tongue—you try!" said the sign under the first mirror. I failed dismally and moved on to the next booth where an equally ridiculous challenge awaited.

About half an hour later, as I reached the end of my journey through the exhibits, I came to a room with a series of windows on one side and a viewing area on the other. To my delight and chagrin, I realized that these windows were the other side of the mirrors I had encountered earlier. Each was filled with an oblivious fellow traveler making a complete fool of himself, much to the delight of the assembled audience.

We humans do strange things when we think no one is watching us!

Morally, however, when we think no one is watching, our true character displays itself. What is on the inside comes out. This comparison of inside-outside, of how who we are affects what we do, is probably the best way to build a framework for the concept of character.

What Does It Really Mean?

The concept of character is often quoted but seldom practiced. Talk is cheap, but doing makes the difference. In this regard, *character* seems to be the forgotten word of our generation. To be fair, it stands little chance in the popularity stakes alongside such power words as *visualization, success, self-esteem,* and *independence.*

True character is not worried about being popular.

True character, however, is not too worried about being popular. Herein lies its strength. Character is about doing what is right, and not necessarily what is convenient or well received. Character is about building an inner world that remains stable and secure, despite external concerns or comforts.

Character separates the mature from the juvenile, the champion from the mediocre, the true leaders from the masses of pretenders. Character cannot be measured by votes, record sales, congregation size, or bank balance. It is both the most needed and the most underrated building block of our society. Character will enable a nation to progress economically while protecting its citizens from social disintegration.

The character vacuum produced by an amoral lifestyle, lack of values, and the pace of modern living can only be filled as people begin to look within rather than without; as they begin to realize that true fulfillment and an authentic sense of significance come not from the applause of man, the enjoyment of life, or the growth of net worth.

> Character remains when materialism and the pursuit of pleasure fail.

When the pursuit of pleasure fails and the myth of materialism becomes self-evident, the essence of character remains and continues to deliver its promises.

Character Defined

The scope and depth of the actual meaning of the word *character* is hard to state simply. Most people understand and have a general feel for the meaning of the word, yet finding a workable definition that encapsulates the power and range of the idea is a difficult task indeed.

Here, then, are a few people's personal definitions of character. Individually, they may not explain all the variations and elements of the elusive word, but, taken as a whole, they are able to explain what could not be made clear were there only one definition.

A man's reputation is only what men think him to be; his character is what God knows him to be.
—Source Unknown

One of the attributes or features that make up and distinguish an individual.
—Merriam-Webster's 11th Collegiate Dictionary

Character is simply habits, long continued.   —Plutarch

Character isn't inherited. One builds it daily by the way one thinks and acts, thought by thought, action by action.   —Helen Mary Gahagan Douglas

The only thing in the world not for sale is character.
                                        —Antonin Scalia

The Paradigm of Being and Doing

Normally, when two strangers meet, the small talk follows a standard procedure. The first question in such circumstances tends to be, "What is your name?" Once introductions have taken place, the inevitable second stage of the relationship is to establish what the other person does. After all, one is what one does.

We are proud of our workplace accomplishments to the degree that most of us derive our identity and self-esteem from what we do. The attendant problems of such a philosophy of life become increasingly evident. Doing takes the place of being. We become driven individuals rather than called individuals. Our evaluation of how life is going is totally dominated by this occupation mentality. Consequently, when retrenchment, retirement, or—worse still—termination and unemployment become our lot, we lose our identity and either drop out, die, or simply become disillusioned. The cry of character would have us change our thinking about who we really are.

Character is all about being; doing is simply the reflection of our inner core. Indeed, true enjoyment in our chosen occupation is a result of doing because of being. Who I am should dictate what I do, not the other way around. In other words, we are human beings not human doings!

When we think no one is watching, our true character displays itself.

When my external world drives me more than the dreams that are within me, I cease to be in charge. Circumstances become my compelling counselors, and my potential to become a world changer is changed by the world.

In his memoirs, Malcolm Muggeridge stated this problem forcibly and hinted at an answer:

> In this Sargasso sea of fantasy and fraud, how can I or anyone else hope to swim unencumbered? How see with, not through, the eye? How take off my own motley, wash away the make-up, raise the iron shutter, put out the studio lights, silence the sound effects and put the cameras to sleep?...Read truth off an autocue, catch it on a screen, chase it on the wings of Muzak? View it in living colour with the news, hear it in living sound along the motorways?...In a still small voice. Not in the screeching of tyres...or in the grinding of brakes; nor in the roar of the jets or the whistle of sirens; not in the howl of trombones, the rattle of drums or the chanting of demo voices. Again, that still small voice—if only one could catch it.[2]

George Bernard Shaw further illustrated this point with great clarity:

The reasonable man adapts himself to the world: the unreasonable one persists in trying to adapt the world to himself. Therefore all progress depends on the unreasonable man.

When I first discovered and mulled over this quotation, it greatly inspired me. We empirically understand that it is all too easy, in this high-pressure world, to be swept along with the tide, to march in time with the majority. We find ourselves inevitably conforming to the values, opinions, and expectations of those who surround us. I believe it was this peer pressure phenomenon that Paul addressed in the New Testament when he wrote, *"Do not conform any longer to the pattern of this world, but be transformed by the renewing of your mind"* (Romans 12:2 NIV). Our personality, character, goals, and aspirations need to be fed from within rather than from without.

> It is all too easy to be swept along with the tide, to march in time with the majority.

But in a world where we are constantly being fed mistruths, doctrines of materialism, and fulfillment of our sinful desires, how can we be sure our inner selves are any better than society at large? This is where the second part of Paul's verse comes in:

Do not conform any longer to the pattern of this world, but be transformed by the renewing of your mind. Then you will be able to test and approve what God's will is—his good, pleasing and perfect will. (verse 2)

Our minds need to be renewed according to a standard outside our natural, limited thinking—the standard of an omnipotent and holy God. He knows what walking on earth is all about, and He has intimate knowledge of a better, higher way. By accepting His guidance over our own, by following His example rather than the world's and allowing Him to be what makes up our "inside," we can know that our insides are better than the world outside.

Inside-out living is what character is all about. Developing an inner superstructure based on a solid Foundation enables us to bring power and security to our outward lives. Suddenly esteem and enthusiasm for life are no longer based on the vagaries of doing, be it employment or recreation, but on the certainty of knowing who we really are on the inside. This has direct ramifications on what we do, how we do it, and why we follow certain courses of action. It is, "I am, therefore I do," not, "I do, therefore I am."

This type of self-analysis is incredibly difficult, as it causes us to confront the most basic of all questions: "Who am I?" Suddenly we discover that we have been using the doing paradigm to divert our attention away from the purpose of our own existence. We often don't want to delve into such matters for fear of what the answer holds. We have been so conditioned by the doctrines of externalism that we begin to doubt that we have anything on the inside at all. The good news, however, for those who have the courage to begin this inward journey, is that this inner world is far richer and fuller than anything we could have dreamed of. We have been, in the words of Zig Ziglar, *"endowed with the seeds of greatness."*

Such existential living is not based on the hope that something lies within but upon the joy and significance that comes from discovering who we really are—God's loved creation.

Developing character will cause our inner lives to be strong and enable us to enjoy external living to the maximum. Doing becomes the overflow of being and, as long as our inner self is growing and focused, our outward living will take care of itself.

The Paradigm of Inward and Outward

"For as [a man] *thinks in his heart, so is he"* (Proverbs 23:7 NKJV).

Outward living should be a reflection of who we are on the inside. Unfortunately the emphasis today is very much on the public person—job, achievements, looks, and assets. Beauty is thought of in terms of physical proportions, success in terms of car model, and life in general in terms of what we have. These small ambitions consume our focus.

Inner growth will always result in external growth.

Character would have us major on the majors and allow the embroidery of life to follow along. Character would beseech us to develop our inner world because eventually it will reflect outward. Our focus must be on the deeper fundamental questions of meaning, purpose, and spirituality. Success and achievement should be inside out. Indeed, one of the great tragedies in the Christian church is the error many established denominations make in concentrating on changing people from the outside in. The Bible speaks of changing the heart, the inner attitudes, the core being of the individual and then allowing that change to work its way to the surface.

After all, it is the love of Christ that will truly change what is inside us, not our own will or ability.

Inner growth will always result in external growth. Who you are—whether you are a businessperson, parent, leader, or Christian—is who you are on the inside well before it becomes apparent on the outside. The hypocrite, of course, is the one whose inner world and outer world do not match at all.

Many live a life of pretense, developing a public image with great vigor and yet failing to give proper attention to the heart. We are made up of three parts: heart (or spirit), mind, and body. With our bodies we relate to the physical world; with our minds, the intellectual world; and with our hearts, the inner dimensions of character and spirituality. Most of us put the bulk of our energy into the mind and body, yet to neglect the heart in order to give attention to the other realms is a decision that lacks insight.

> Character is about what we have on the inside—who we really are.

Pascal's phrase, *"Pious scholars rare,"* probably has this in mind. What he meant, I believe, is that any individual who becomes a master in one dimension of life rarely gives time or thought to the others. Herbert Butterfield had the same truth in mind when he penned these words:

> Both in history and in life it is a phenomenon by no means rare to meet with comparatively unlettered people who seem to have struck profound spiritual depths...while there are many highly educated people of whom one feels they are performing clever antics with their minds to cover a gaping hollowness that lies within.[3]

It is not letters (or scholarly degrees) that matter; it is our heart. Character is about what we have on the inside—who we really are. This book is about exploring this inner world and learning how to develop and change our inner selves in order to experience authentic and successful living. We will discover that, in attempting to structure our private worlds by building positive character qualities, we will often need help, not only from our friends, but also from God. Character, it seems, cannot be completely self-generated. We all need a perspective and strength greater than ourselves. We have the ability to recognize our need for change, but we lack the necessary power to accomplish the task.

My prayer is that, as you begin to look at specific character qualities, you will identify the problem, decide on the solution, and reach out to the only Power that can really change the hidden person of the heart.

The Super Achiever is a person of authentic essence and solid character.

This book is written to the person who desires to achieve and grow in life. It is for the kind of person who is not content to simply exist but has a sense of destiny, an inner awareness that, despite the pain of this world, he is meant to be part of the solution. It is for the person who knows that there is a job to do and that just living for the weekend and looking forward to retirement, without developing the inner resources of the heart, is the highest form of selfishness.

I believe that if we purpose to do what is necessary to make these secrets of Super Achievers our own, we will transform our lives, inside and out.

We must first, however, define our terms. If definitions differ on what being a Super Achiever really is, then, no doubt, expectations may go unfulfilled.

The Super Achiever cannot be defined in a mere positional or financial way. The Super Achiever is not the fabulously wealthy person with the broken marriage, or the respected leader caught in a prison of personal, compulsive, self-destructive habits.

The term is used holistically and covers not only our financial and career world but also the relational, social, mental, physical, and spiritual worlds. The Super Achiever is a person not just of accomplishment but of authentic essence and solid character. All these things are, of course, inextricably intertwined.

Most of the chapters that follow have to do with character traits that must be nurtured and developed. This is paramount to achieving our goal of success in life. Skills, techniques, and practices are of secondary importance. There is a plethora of books available in today's marketplace that deal with such things. Our purpose, however, is to get at the heart of the problem and, therefore, to the heart of the answer—for that is where the journey begins.

JUST A PUPPET ON A STRING

Responsibility

"As human beings, we are endowed with freedom of choice, and we cannot shuffle off our responsibility upon the shoulders of God or nature. We must shoulder it ourselves. It is up to us."

Arnold J. Toynbee

Chapter Two

Just a Puppet on a String

Our culture has become one of complaint, blame, and non-responsibility. Everything is someone else's fault, and excuses are the morphine of our time. The legal profession has thrived on our belief in this lie, as our sue-happy society illustrates. We pay for it, too, not only through our insurance rates but also with our souls. The teaching "I am not to blame" has grown in popularity, especially in the last forty years. It has been sustained by our willingness to believe it, fueled by Freudian psychology, and now it is fanned white-hot by the genetic arguments put forth as excuses for every type of human behavior and misbehavior. To be consistent, then, we should also never claim credit for victories won or goals achieved.

Our culture has become one of non-responsibility.

The blame mentality, if correct, would declare that nothing good or bad is ever our own fault. This type of fatalism does not wash with most people, so we moderate the harsh reality of taking it to its logical conclusion and develop an irrational philosophy of life—a philosophy that says we are the reason for our successes and others are the reason for our failures. Zig Ziglar has pointed out that we have all heard of the self-made success but never the self-made failure.

Fighting the Blame Mentality

Super Achievers fight the human tendency to blame others with every fiber of their beings. They take responsibility for their own lives. They are humble in victory and reflective in defeat. Winston Churchill once said, *"Responsibility is the price of greatness."* The sooner you accept that the number one person responsible for all your woes is yourself, the quicker you will begin to make decisions that will change your life.

Gordon Gray once said, *"If you could kick the person responsible for most of your troubles, you wouldn't be able to sit down for six months!"*

Time is not an endless, inevitable cycle where history repeats itself and the individual has no influence or control. Time is a line: It has a beginning and an end, and it moves in a particular direction. In living our lives, it is important to understand that we are not caught in some kind of meaningless cosmic whirlpool where the events and circumstances we all face each day are controlling our futures and causing us to be the people we are.

> Our choices are significant, and our futures are flexible.

No! Life is more like a river. We can allow ourselves to go with the flow and see where the various currents take us, but we also have enough control to either paddle to the bank or move upstream. To be responsible for ourselves is to realize that our choices are significant—what we do affects who we are and where we will end up. In short, our futures are flexible.

An awareness of the role we play in our own lives is essential if we are to move away from the victim mentality.

John Maxwell, in his book *Developing the Leader Within You* includes some research conducted with prison inmates:

> A psychologist visited a prison and asked various inmates, "Why are you here?" The answers were very revealing, even though expected. There were many of them: "I was framed;" "They ganged up on me;" "It was a case of mistaken identity."
>
> The psychologist wondered if one could possibly find a larger group of "innocent" people anywhere else but in prison![4]

Probably the best story I have heard illustrating the principle of responsibility is the following:

> The sales manager of a dog food company asked his salespeople how they liked the company's new advertising program.
>
> "Great! Best in the business!" the salespeople responded.
>
> "How do you like our new label and package?"
>
> "Great! Best in the business!" the salespeople responded.
>
> "How do you like our sales force?"
>
> They were the sales force. They had to admit they were good.
>
> "Okay, then," said the manager, "So we've got the best label, the best package, and the best advertising program being sold by the best sales force in the business. Tell me why we are in seventeenth place in the dog food business?"
>
> There was silence. Finally someone said, "It's those lousy dogs. They won't eat the stuff!"[5]

Others can slow us down or even try to put roadblocks on the way to our potential, but we are the only ones who can stop the car or change direction. Super Achievers take control of their lives. They refuse to accept that their culture, heritage, net worth, physical appearance, and education (or lack of it) controls their lives. Only desire, decision, and determination are important.

> Super Achievers take control of their lives.

Four Exceptions to the Rule

There are of course some exceptions to this law of responsibility. In fact, there are four:

Number One—Only Child

Only children have life pretty rough. Absence of sibling rivalry in the formative years often allows pride and self-centeredness to creep in. The necessity of sharing and giving are lessons poorly learned by the only child. So, when the time comes to enter the rough-and-tumble of life outside the domestic situation, they are ill prepared for what follows and cannot, by virtue of their upbringing, be truly successful in life.

Number Two—Middle Child

The middle child has a different set of problems to deal with. The parents boast about the oldest child and spoil the youngest, often forgetting all about the one in between.

"This is Tom our eldest, and darling Sally our youngest, and this is...I'm sorry, I've forgotten your name!" The resulting inferiority complex practically guarantees a lack of achievement in the middle child's life.

Number Three—Youngest Child

The baby of the family shares many of the problems of the only child, as well as the extra pressures of parents tired of parenting and elder brothers and sisters who resent the resulting breakdown of all previous house rules, regulations, and curfews. The result is that this child lacks the ability to develop strong character in areas critical for future success and significance.

Number Four—The Eldest Child

If you thought the previous three had problems, they are nothing compared to the firstborn. Not only do firstborns come into the world when their parents are the least experienced, but also when they are most financially disadvantaged. Thus they endure parental experimentation and become guinea pigs for failure after failure. When they finally realize what is going on, the parents have a change of heart and modify all the rules for their younger brothers and sisters. It's just not fair!

The Point

My point is, one's upbringing can be used as either an excuse for failure or a reason for success. Your family, like so many others, may have been dysfunctional, but you must learn to break free. We need to be mature. We need to take responsibility. Only then will we be on the road to true significance.

DAZE OF OUR LIVES
Overriding Goal or Passion

"You will become as small as your controlling desire; as great as your dominant aspiration."

James Allen

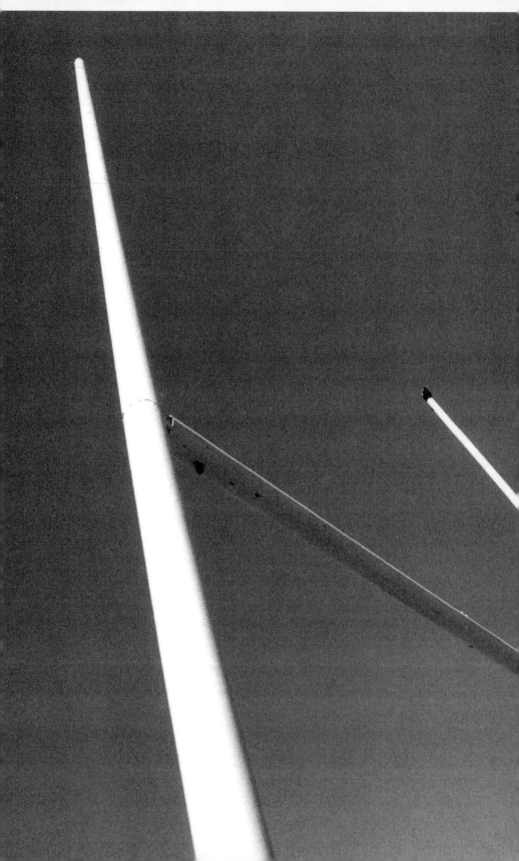

Chapter Three

Daze of Our Lives

Life for the Super Achiever is not about doing many things but about accomplishing one thing: a purpose so compelling that one could call it a life goal. All other goals fit within the framework of this life goal. This one purpose, this one passion, gives the Super Achiever a sense of direction and a point of reference. Pursuits, desires, invitations, and opportunities are all either consciously or subconsciously sifted through the perspective of the one overriding purpose.

We only have to think of the Super Achievers throughout history to realize that all of them had a singular purpose that was uppermost in their minds. Other challenges overcome and smaller achievements accomplished in the early years were seen as preparation for the major mission.

On May 10, 1940, in the first part of World War II, Winston Churchill became prime minister. He described it thus:

> I was conscious of a profound sense of relief. At last I had the authority to give directions over the whole scene. I felt as if I were walking with Destiny, and that all my past life had been but preparation for this hour and for this trial.

In the New Testament the apostle Paul talked about *"this one thing I do"* (Philippians 3:13 KJV). Jesus had a single mission: to die for His people and become their sacrifice for sin. The heart of Martin Luther King Jr. cried for freedom and equality at every opportunity. Gandhi's clarion call was independence for India. Mother Teresa did her "one thing" in pursuing the call and example of Christ, and now countless disciples are following in her footsteps.

When we, as individuals, come to terms with this truth, many of us become painfully aware, almost immediately, that we have been living fragmented lives. We attempt to move in opposite directions at the same time. We float wherever the current takes us, believing that wherever we end up will be the right destination.

If one is to make a difference in one's world, there must be an overall sense of direction.

The life of the Super Achiever argues against this way of thinking. His testimony is echoed by the quiet voice of his own heart. Somehow, deep within us, we know that if one is to reach greatness, if one is to make a difference in one's world, there must be an overall sense of direction. There must be commitment, enthusiasm, and effort. There must be a willingness to go against the majority; to fight against the tides of apathy and mediocrity; to pursue, with passion, the reason we have been created.

Intuitively we also realize that, with the discovery of life purpose, there comes a general sense of contentment, fulfillment, and even serenity. Pervading despair, loss of personal peace, and the overall confusion of life are rare maladies among Super Achievers.

The film *City Slickers* illustrates this principle. The character played by Billy Crystal, having arrived at middle age, is trying to find his smile again. Crystal and his friends decide to go on a cattle drive as a means of rediscovering themselves, where they are confronted with a simple yet penetrating truth. Crystal asks the old cattleman leading the group, "What is the secret of life?" The cattleman answers, "Just one thing." When Crystal responds by asking what this one thing could be, the answer, "That's what you've got to find out," stops him in his tracks.

Super Achievers have found their one thing. They spend their lives pursuing it with a tenacity and discipline that can only be caused by discovered destiny.

The defining call of the Super Achiever is of a far higher intensity than the regular, yet ever-changing, plans and dreams of everyday folk.

There are certain characteristics that qualify an ambition, goal, or purpose to be the "one thing."

Bigger than Oneself

First, it is important to have a life goal that is bigger than oneself; to have a cause that goes beyond personal wealth and satisfaction. We need causes that will touch the lives of others and bring meaning to our work. It is not enough to just pay the bills, buy the Learjet, or spend one's life playing golf in the world's best resorts. The idle rich have their rewards, but they are nothing compared to those of the Super Achiever.

I am in a peculiar position. No one can give me anything. There is nothing I want that I cannot have. But I do not want the things that money can buy. I want to live a life, to make the world a little better for having lived in it.[6]
—Henry Ford

The miser who lives for himself dies miserably. I am reminded of one such man who, as he reached the end of his days, decided to try to cheat the old maxim, *"You can't take it with you."*

Summoning his lawyer, doctor, and minister to his bedside, he entrusted to each an envelope containing $100,000 cash.

"I have no friends, and you gentlemen are the only ones I can trust," he said. "What I have given you is the sum total of my life's savings. I want you each to swear a solemn pledge to throw your envelope with its money into my grave when they begin to bury me."

The three men agreed to fulfill this task, and about a month later the old miser died.

We need causes that will touch the lives of others and bring meaning to our work.

When the first clods fell onto the coffin, so too did the three envelopes as the doctor, lawyer, and minister stood seriously at the graveside. After the funeral, the three decided to join each other for a drink. It wasn't long before the doctor spoke up. "Sirs, I have to confess. My practice has been difficult, my wife has developed a serious drinking problem, and money has been in short supply. I took $30,000 out of my envelope and only threw in $70,000."

There was a moment's silence, and then the lawyer began to speak. "I too must get this off my chest. These last twelve months have been very difficult for me. I have developed a gambling addiction that has almost destroyed my life. I took out $70,000 and only threw in $30,000."

The minister, as you can well imagine, was shocked by these admissions. He stood up and addressed both men. "Gentlemen, I cannot believe you have broken your pledges in this manner. I want you both to know that I threw in a check for the full amount!"

Making an Impact

The life purpose, the goal, the consuming passion, must be something that impacts the lives of others in positive ways.

I believe that it was this very fact that caused John Sculley, then CEO of PepsiCo, to move to Apple Computer. Negotiations were failing to entice him across to the new maverick computer firm. It was becoming apparent to Steve Jobs, one of the founders of Apple, that he could not offer Sculley anything he did not already have, especially when it came to profit sharing, salary, retirement plan, or any of the perks that would go with such a position.

> The lie of our culture is that a "me first" philosophy is the key to success.

The deal was clinched when Jobs had almost given up hope. A simple statement, *"Well, do you want to spend the rest of your life selling sugared water or do you want a chance to change the world?"* challenged Sculley to think about the bigger picture. He realized that the power of a life mission that would impact the world was infinitely greater than all the possessions and respectability money could buy.

In this light, we can see why the philosophy of hedonism fails. The self-absorbed life, the life intent upon personal pleasure as its primary goal, will always lead to disillusionment and finally to despair.

The self-obsessed life cannot lead to inner meaning, serenity, or any sense of significance. The lie of our culture is that a "me first" philosophy is the key to success. However, even a cursory look at what brings prosperity and achievement in any endeavor begins to show that self-absorption is a sure path to failure.

> The self-obsessed life cannot lead to any sense of significance.

A sporting team must work together, serving one another. A business needs to harness power through synergy. A good leader must serve those he is called to lead. Christ, of course, was the ultimate example of putting others first. By His death and by His life, He taught that loving and honoring God and His people is the key to one's own fruitfulness and fulfillment.

Success comes to those who use it to bless others. Success is God's way of helping other people. The businessperson who is trying to be successful just for himself will never compare with the one who has a bigger goal: the goal of reaching out to touch the lives of others.

We are wired to find our greatest fulfillment and joy in using who we are and what we have to benefit those around us. It has been said that one quickly finds the falseness of materialism and hedonism by attempting to live them out. Those who give their lives to God discover they are living life at its deepest and most rewarding level.

You Love It!

Your chances of success are directly proportional to the degree of pleasure you desire from what you do. If you are in a job you hate, face the fact squarely and get out. —Michael Korda

One of the brightest signposts to destiny is love. Often the decision to change career paths from the well paying but boring job to a riskier endeavor that fires the soul opens the way to unrealized potential.

One of the brightest signposts to destiny is love.

Isaac Asimov, the science fiction writer, is a case in point. Leaving the secure position of college professor, he became one of the most successful writers of modern time, with over 470 books published.

Vincent van Gogh, who left Christian ministry to paint simply because he loved it, made this point clearly in one of his letters:

In my opinion, I am often rich as Croesus—not in money, but (though it doesn't happen every day) rich—because I have found in my work something which I can devote myself to heart and soul, and which inspires me and gives a meaning to life.

It has been well said that most die with their music still in them. This is probably because they never give themselves wholeheartedly to what they love to do or, worse still, because that love alludes them all their lives.

Love and destiny go hand in hand. We are wired with both purpose and passion. When we discover one, we will find the other.

Discovered, Not Chosen

I refuse to believe the notion that man is flotsam and jetsam in the river of life, unable to influence the unfolding events which surround him.
—Dr. Martin Luther King Jr.

A third characteristic of the life-reorienting goal is that it is discovered rather than chosen. Intuition here is far more important than analysis. We must look deep within the recesses of our souls to find out how we have been made. What gets me excited? What gets me angry? What do I dream about? What would I do if I could do anything? If I knew it was impossible for me to fail, what would I attempt? What gifts and talents do I have, even in an embryonic stage, that if developed to their potential could make a difference to this world?

Life goals have a sense of predestination about them. When people finally reach the point when they say, "This is what I choose to do with my life," they are also aware that somehow their lives were chosen to do this. They find, as a result, that they are not driving themselves toward a goal but are operating out of a deep sense of calling.

Churchill's words, quoted earlier, give us the impression that, when he found his life's purpose, he was aware, at the deepest level, that he was not deciding to do this but, rather, that the decision had already been made. He was meant to do this. This revelation may have come to him in a sudden flash, a eureka moment, and in his case, late in life. On the other hand, it may have developed as a deep sense of knowing from an early age. Only he knows. Regardless of how one comes to the understanding of purpose, it is vitally important that we believe that there is such a purpose and that we spend our lives looking, asking, and expecting its sudden or slow arrival. Perhaps it may be that, while reading these very words, you find a deep stirring within your heart, a realization that you have been satisfied with the status quo and settled for mediocrity. The time has come to be desperate enough to search, find, and follow the dream of your heart and the intended purpose of your soul.

YOU HAVE TO JUMP IN THE PUDDLES

Optimism

"The higher you go in any organization of value, the better the attitude you'll find."

John Maxwell

Chapter Four

You Have to Jump in the Puddles

Super Achievers tend to be highly optimistic people. Not only do they believe in others, but their view of life is that things are somehow going to work out their way. This perspective pervades every part of their beings.

Optimism is all about having a positive outlook, maintaining a sense of humor, and developing long-term hope.

Positive Outlook

Helen Keller declared, *"Life is a daring adventure or it is nothing."* Super Achievers would agree. They tend naturally to see the best rather than the worst. They are the kind of people who are genuinely disappointed when they don't win the door prize; they truly expect the best possible things to happen to them.

A positive outlook is more than smiling in the face of problems or simplistically pretending that things are not as bad as they really are. Optimism is a deep inner belief that, despite everything, there is more going for you than against you. It is believing that love, hope, and integrity, while not always appearing to win in the external circumstances of life, build an inner strength that far outshines the alternative.

"*Without minimizing catastrophe, the consistent and astonishing result is that the worst emotional consequences of bad events are usually temporary,*" writes social psychologist David G. Myers.

> Searching for the positive is the surest and speediest path to growth.

His comment is based on the attitude and inner world of the one suffering. Looking beyond the immediate and searching for the positive is the surest and speediest path to both recuperation and growth. Myers continues by citing the example of W. Mitchell:

> *In 1971 he was horribly burned, nearly killed, and left fingerless from a freak motorcycle accident. Four years later tragedy struck again. This time he was paralyzed from the waist down in a small plane crash. Though terribly disfigured, he chose not to buy the idea that happiness requires handsomeness. "I am in charge of my own spaceship. It is my up, my down. I could choose to see this situation as a setback or a starting point." Mitchell today is a successful investor, an environmental activist, and a speaker who encourages people to step back from their own misfortunes: "Take a wider view and say, 'Maybe that isn't such a big thing after all!'"*[7]

Dark pessimism, as a philosophy of life, leads to despair, depression, and cynicism. Those who take this perspective fail to see, much less admire, the rainbows of life. Their attention is on the storm. Dr. Denis Waitley says, "*Losers see the icy streets; winners put on their ice skates.*" The pessimist's light at the end of the tunnel is the oncoming train, and his stubborn refusal to believe anything else locks him into a vicious cycle of self-fulfilling prophecy.

Optimism, however, still grits its teeth at life's difficulties, but it does so with a slight smile on its face.

It has been said, *"Adversity will either wear you down or polish you up."* Those who are negative in life only see the problems. When opportunity knocks, they complain about the noise. Their glass of water is half empty because they are draining the water away. The optimist, on the other hand, is solution conscious. She is adding to the water level and excited about the future. She is quick to follow Henry Ford's dictum, *"Don't find fault, find a remedy."*

The optimist is solution conscious.

The Super Achiever is hardly ever the somber, intense, overly melancholic individual. Rather, he tends to have a sparkle in his eye, a skip in his step, and a sense of play and wonder.

In this, we can learn a lot from children. Indeed, we can learn a lot from remembering ourselves when we were children. Remember laughing out loud at everyday occurrences you don't even notice now? Remember jumping in puddles when it rained and being careful not to walk on the cracks?

I think, as adults, we should jump in more puddles rather than complain about the rain. We should sing more and smile more. We should take time to smell the flowers, look at the view, and enjoy the journey.

We rush lemming-like through life, frustrated at red lights, impatient in elevators, and hassled by long lines. Life will always have its puddles and red lights, but they are there to be enjoyed. They are welcome distractions and breaks in the rush hour of life.

While I am writing this, I am sitting at a sidewalk café. The rain has started to fall, much to the delight of a small, two-year-old girl. She is standing outside, face upward, trying to catch a few raindrops in her mouth, and I...I am upset that my notes are getting wet!

Optimism, in one sense, doesn't change anything, but, in another sense, it changes everything. Life is not about what happens to you but about how you react to it. The Super Achiever realizes there is always something in life to be thankful for. The serious view of life, even if it may be more realistic at times, is not as much fun, and fun is necessary to sabotage stress, diffuse frustration, and maximize productivity.

Sense of Humor

Ogden Nash once wrote,

It is better in the long run to possess an abscess or a tumor than to possess a sense of humor.
People who have senses of humor have a very good time
But they never accomplish anything of note, either despicable or sublime.
Because how can anyone accomplish anything immortal
When they realize they look pretty funny doing it and have to stop and chortle?[8]

Ogden Nash was wrong!

While great leaders in any area are rarely comedians, they do share the ability to laugh at life and at themselves. Being able to see the funny side is often what enables the Super Achiever to endure with grace and move smoothly through life's difficult spots. Humor is the oil that reduces the friction of great responsibility.

Winston Churchill is one of my favorites in this regard. There are several well-known stories that illustrate this principle in his life.

As prime minister during the war years, Churchill was lauded for his speeches, but not by all. A certain woman took much delight in continually disagreeing with him. She once remarked, *"If you were my husband, I would poison your tea."* To which Churchill responded, *"Madame, if you were my wife, I would drink it."*

Laughing during life's journey improves the view.

On another occasion, George Bernard Shaw sent Churchill a letter containing tickets. The letter read:

I am enclosing two tickets to the first night of my new play, bring a friend—if you have one.

Churchill returned the tickets the following day with a letter of his own.

Cannot possibly attend first night, will attend second—if there is one.

Religious people have a tendency to be intense, serious, and often lacking in humor. The Pharisees who accosted Jesus were such individuals. Yet those who walk with God in an authentic way are quick to smile. No wonder Malcolm

Muggeridge chose the title *Something Beautiful for God* for his biography of Mother Teresa.

A vibrant sense of humor is an attribute of God Himself. Laughing during life's journey improves the view and reduces the stress. James Thurber wrote, *"Laughter need not be cut out of anything, since it improves everything."*

Sense of Hope

Loss of hope is the problem of our age. Progressively, the foundations of society have been undermined; hope is the last to fall. One author put it this way:

In the 1950s, kids lost their innocence. They were liberated from their parents by well-paying jobs, cars, and lyrics in music that gave rise to a new term—the generation gap.

In the 1960s, kids lost their authority. It was the decade of protest—church, state, parents were all called into question and found wanting. Their authority was rejected, yet nothing ever replaced it.

In the 1970s, kids lost their love. It was the decade of me-ism, dominated by hyphenated words beginning with self: self-image, self-esteem, self-assertion. It made for a lonely world. Kids learned everything there was to know about sex but forgot everything there was to know about love, and no one had the nerve to tell them the difference.

In the 1980s, kids lost their hope. Stripped of innocence, authority and love, and plagued by the horror of a nuclear nightmare, large and growing numbers of their generation stopped believing in the future.[9]

Hope is essential for life itself. Despair leads to death. This is why the inscription *"All hope abandon, all ye who enter here"* at the entrance to hell in Dante's *Inferno* is so damning.

Hope is essential for life itself.

The Super Achiever not only maintains hopes but usually has an active plan to develop them as well. She believes in getting her hopes up. Such hope in life, in the future, is an absolute prerequisite to successful endeavor in any field. Even in the pragmatic area of economics, the power of hope, along with its legitimate child, faith, cannot be undervalued. As George Gilder, writer for the *Wall Street Journal*, points out:

Faith in man, faith in the future, faith in the rising returns of giving, faith in the mutual benefits of trade, faith in the providence of God are all essential to successful capitalism. All are necessary to sustain the spirit of work and enterprise against the setbacks and frustrations it inevitably meets in a fallen world; to inspire trust and cooperation in an economy where they will often be betrayed; to encourage the forgoing of present pleasures in the name of a future that may well go up in smoke; to promote risk and initiative in a world where the rewards all vanish unless others join the game. In order to give without the assurance of return, in order to save without the certainty of future value, in order to work beyond the requirements of the job, one has to have confidence in a higher morality: a law of compensations beyond the immediate and distracting struggles of existence.[10]

There is a dimension to hope that we don't often think about, and that is the sense of hope produced not by the expectation of a favorable outcome but rather by the sense of purpose we have in what we are doing, regardless of outcome.

Vaclav Havel, the brilliant and compassionate president of the Czech Republic, has seen this more clearly than most. For many years, he was an opposition writer whose protests in the name of human rights landed him in jail several times. In the face of an all-controlling communist government, he held on to hope because he was convinced, not of the final victory his ideas would have, but simply that they were right and true:

> I should probably say first that the kind of hope I often think about (especially in situations that are particularly hopeless, such as prison) I understand above all as a state of mind, not a state of the world. Either we have hope within us or we don't; it is a dimension of the soul, and it's not essentially dependent on some particular observation of the world or estimate of the situation. Hope is not prognostication....
>
> Hope, in this deep and powerful sense, is not the same as joy that things are going well, or willingness to invest in enterprises that are obviously headed for success, but, rather, an ability to work for something because it is good, not just because it stands a chance to succeed. The more unpropitious the situation in which we demonstrate hope, the deeper that hope is. Hope is definitely not the same thing as optimism. It is not the conviction that something will turn out well, but the certainty that something makes sense, regardless of how it turns out.[11]

Viktor E. Frankl recorded one of the best-known examples of such remarkable hope. His book *Man's Search for Meaning* was a product of the Nazi concentration camps. Dr. Frankl spent three years as a prisoner in four different camps. He observed and felt the extremities of human suffering.

We must work to keep our hopes up.

He discovered the only thing that kept the condemned alive was hope. One of his favorite quotes was from Nietzsche: *"He who has a why to live for can bear with almost any how."*

It was this "why" that gave rise to the hope that sustained life as its darkest hour.

Frankl recounts a talk he gave to a group of fellow prisoners on this very point:

> *I asked the poor creatures who listened to me attentively in the darkness of the hut to face the seriousness of our position. They must not lose hope but should keep their courage in the certainty that the hopelessness of our struggle did not detract from its dignity and its meaning. I said that someone looks down on each of us in difficult hours—a friend, a wife, somebody alive or dead, or a God—and he would not expect us to disappoint him. He would hope to find us suffering proudly—not miserably—knowing how to die.*[12]

Hope can begin to dissipate simply through the process of aging, and thus cannot be simply taken for granted. We must work to keep our hopes up.

Every time I go to a funeral, I am confronted with the inevitable end of the mortal road. It never used to grab me, but now, as the years roll by, I begin to sense its presence. It seems that the older we are, the sadder we are at such occasions. We mourn for ourselves, as well as for the deceased. We bid adieu to one who has finished while bearing the inescapable knowledge that one day it will be us. Our time will come, and young men and women will follow our caskets and then return to their lives. For them, their day is far away, as it was once for us.

It is not only possible but essential to build hope as we get older. This may seem difficult in the face of such an inescapable conclusion as death. Still, there is One who came back from the other side, and my faith, love, and hope are founded upon Him.

FATAL DISTRACTION

Focus

"Every great man has become great, every successful man has succeeded, in proportion as he has confined his powers to one particular channel."

Orison Swett Marden

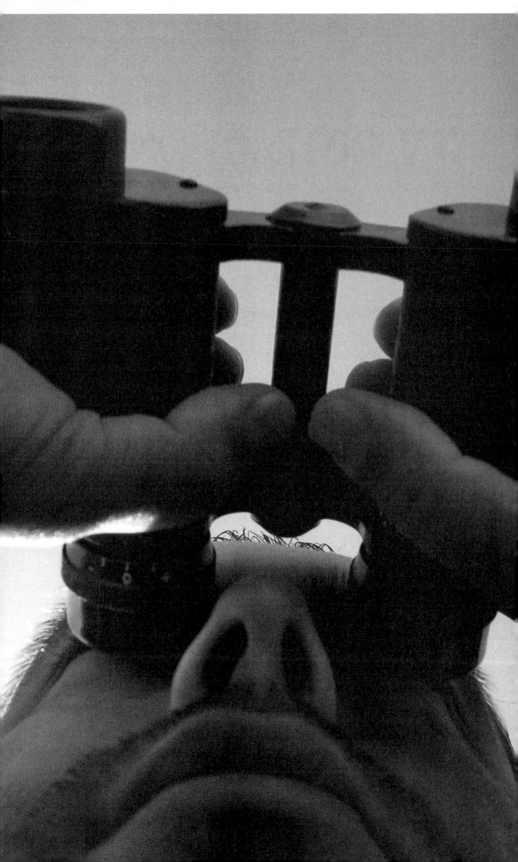

Chapter Five

Fatal Distraction

Super Achievers have learned the importance of focus and concentration, and they refuse to be led astray by interesting yet fatal distractions.

> *Racing is all I want to do. I don't have a Plan A and a Plan B.* —Mario Andretti

Chet Atkins, member of the country music hall of fame, puts it this way:

> *Maybe there are a few shortcuts for a rock star who becomes an overnight sensation and is forgotten about tomorrow. But you take a guy like Glen Campbell, who's a very good guitarist, or Roy Clark, a great entertainer, or Jerry Reed. They spent twelve hours a day for many years playing the guitar. They may tell you different, but they did. Everybody does. I took the guitar with me to the bathroom, everywhere I went, I played it—because I loved it. Jerry Reed says, "You gotta be eat up with it! You've got to love it with a passion that will follow you to the grave....If you don't have that, you might as well forget it, I think."[13]*

The realization of one's life goal is all-important. It is both primary and paramount in becoming a Super Achiever because from this discovery flow the other characteristics required to reach our potential. The first result in discovering our calling, as it were, is that we find our lives become focused. The capacity to concentrate on the important things rather than the superficial is a direct result of knowing where we are going. Focus enables us to control our consciousness, to guard our hearts, and to protect our minds. We must have this type of protection against causes, ambitions, and other fascinations, which may not be harmful in the final analysis but, by their very existence, cause us to get sidetracked and lose momentum.

The ability to concentrate always brings results. Whether we are talking about concentrating on an exam, making it through a negotiation process, or winning the love of your life, concentration yields fruit. Such focus harnesses all our powers at once. Zig Ziglar gives the analogy of holding a magnifying glass, in the heat of the day, over a pile of dry leaves. If we keep moving the magnifying glass, we will never create the heat necessary to start the fire. However, the moment we hold it stationary, allowing the light and heat of the sun to focus on one small part of the foliage, the leaves will quickly burst into flame.

> The ability to concentrate always brings results.

Why is it that a life of focus brings such great rewards? There are two major reasons. One has to do with motivation; the other with simplicity.

Motivation

First of all, focus unleashes the necessary motivation that moves you toward your life mission. There should be no surprise regarding the fact that success in life is all about such things as attitude, consistency, character, and motivation. Without such traits, the competent, the able, and the geniuses will fall far behind. William Ward put it this way:

Enthusiasm and persistence can make an average person superior. Indifference and lethargy can make a superior person average.

Simple laziness is all too often unfairly blamed. Lethargy is more a symptom, not a cause, of failure in life. My favorite quotation on the subject of laziness is by Spike Milligan:

Well, we can't stand around here doing nothing; people will think we are workmen.

The truth is, however, most people are not lazy; they are simply uninspired. Motivation comes from having a goal that is inspirational. This, in turn, causes us to focus our lives even more and gives us the energy with which we can accomplish our dreams.

> Most people are not lazy; they are simply uninspired.

The goal becomes both the target and the fuel.
                                          —Dr. Denis Waitley

Not all motivation is necessarily good motivation. There are several different types:

Fear Motivation

Fear motivation is motivation in its lowest form. Fear motivation involves doing something because we don't like the consequences of not doing it. It is often used by parents to motivate children and by teachers to motivate their pupils. Employers have attempted to use it with questionable results. "Firings will continue until morale improves!" Fear motivation works for a little while but will usually produce such by-products as resentment and bitterness; it is, at best, effective only over the short-term.

I am reminded of a man who tried to lose weight by using this type of motivation. He called it the blackmail diet! He created fear motivation for himself by placing all his savings into a trust account that would be payable to a neo-Nazi party if he did not lose forty-five pounds by the end of the year. The dread of losing his money, and giving it to an organization he despised, was sufficient motivation to reach his goal.

Incentive Motivation

The next level of motivation is incentive motivation. This involves doing something because of the rewards that become ours when we do it.

"Whoever reaches the number one spot this month will be sent on an all-expense-paid vacation to Bali" and "If you clean your room tonight, you can stay up and watch an extra half hour of television" are both examples of incentive motivation. The old carrot in front of the donkey does seem to get things done. The problem arises, however, when the donkey gets bored with the carrot or simply has had enough to eat.

Internal Motivation

The third type is the highest form of motivation. It involves doing something because we want to do it, despite the penalties of not doing it or the rewards for achieving it. This is an energy that comes from within and moves us forward. We achieve because we believe. We have it within ourselves to get the job done.

An easily understood example is found in the film *Rocky III*. Rocky decides to get his title back, not to regain the respect he has lost or for financial rewards, but simply because he wants it for himself. He is thus enabled to face his fears and come out of the bout having won the inner fight, self-respect intact.

We achieve because we believe.

One key secret of Super Achievers is that they have this kind of motivation. They keep on knocking on the doors when everyone else has given up. They have a stubbornness that goes beyond the norm, and they have the ability to believe they will get the job done just because they know they are somehow meant to. This knowing that they are meant to motivates them from the inside out.

It is this motivation that causes martyrs to sacrifice their lives and missionaries to give up the comforts of home. They are motivated by a love for God that surpasses any desire for earthly comforts, or even for life. It is God who can give this sort of purpose and mission. Whether He calls you to the mission field or to start a new business right in your hometown, when He calls you, there is no going back.

Simplicity

I have only one purpose, the destruction of Hitler, and my life is much simplified thereby. If Hitler invaded Hell,

---

*I would make at least a favorable reference to the Devil
in the House of Commons.* —Winston Churchill

The focused life also enables maximum energy and time to be put toward the primary goal. It simplifies life in order to fulfill the task at hand.

So often, those who do not achieve in life are wasting time and energy in a multitude of tasks and pursuits. This type of approach, at best, normally results in mediocrity or mere competence. Excellence, however, belongs to those who would do nothing else. The Super Achiever refuses to allow the urgent to replace the important.

> Simplicity enables us to know what we should overlook.

Simplicity enables us to know what we should overlook. This planned neglect of things outside our field of vision can and will yield great reward.

The man who seeks one thing in life and but one,
May hope to achieve it before life is done;
But he who seeks all things, wherever he goes
Only reaps from the hopes which around him he sows
A harvest of barren regrets.[14]

The ability to *"lay aside every weight...[and] run with endurance the race that is set before us"* (Hebrews 12:1 NKJV) is a direct result of a focused life. The Super Achiever realizes that diversions may be interesting in their own right, but the sidetrack they inevitably present will simply delay or even destroy the sense of direction and commitment that is central to the road of significance. Such simplicity helps us make full use of our allotted time.

Benjamin Franklin said, *"Dost thou love life? Then do not squander time because that is the stuff life is made of."* John F. Kennedy said, *"We must use time as a tool not as a couch."*

The focused life, then, is both a simple life (in the sense of direction) and a motivated one. Weeks may pass with few visible results, but momentum is building and, inevitably, destiny will become reality.

IT'S NOT CHECKOUT TIME YET

Endurance

6

"Never, never, never, never give up."

Winston Churchill

Chapter Six

It's Not Checkout Time Yet

Achieving
in life is not just about being in the right place at the right time; it's also about being in the wrong place at the wrong time and not giving up. Greatness is often born in the cauldron of suffering and pain, where the abilities to maintain perspective and walk in forgiveness are learned. It is in the hard places, the lonely places, that we discover whether or not we really have an all-consuming purpose or sense of destiny.

Super Achievers respond to pain differently from other people. They do not look for escape but for lessons. They get better rather than bitter. They realize that, in the words of Robert Schuller, *"Tough times don't last, tough people do."* More than that, they see pain and trial as prerequisites for the character lessons that must be learned if destiny is to be reached. Churchill learned patience and persistence in his wilderness years between the wars. Kennedy's suffering at the Bay of Pigs, when the plan to depose Castro came unstuck, was the right kind of preparation for the Cuban Missile Crisis.

The achievement of one's goal in life does not come at a discounted price. It is high, and many people refuse to pay it. The Super Achiever, however, realizes that, before victory, there is battle; before resurrection, a cross. You cannot have one without the other.

William Penn once said, *"No pain, no palm; no thorns, no throne; no gall, no glory; no cross, no crown."* When Jesus came to earth, He knew the pain and trial He'd have to undergo. But He came anyway because He also knew the joy and glory His death would bring us into. Furthermore, He knew that, while His pain on earth would be temporary, His reign in heaven would be eternal.

The achievement of one's goal doesn't come at a discounted price.

Helen Keller, who certainly had her fair share of pain and problems, wrote, *"Character cannot be developed in ease and quiet. Only through experience of trial and suffering can the soul be strengthened, vision cleared, ambition inspired, and success achieved."*

It would be wrong to surmise from the preceding paragraphs that our reaction to tests should be one of acceptance and passivity. The very word *endurance* has in it the concept of fighting and resisting. A stoic attitude toward life may be effective against anxiety, but it does not, at the same time, achieve destiny. No, the one who achieves his destiny must cling to the dream and, with every fiber of his being, go to battle. Hamlet's soliloquy brilliantly contrasts the active versus the passive view of overcoming obstacles:

> *To be or not to be: that is the question:*
> *Whether 'tis nobler in the mind to suffer*
> *The slings and arrows of outrageous fortune,*
> *Or to take arms against a sea of troubles,*
> *And by opposing, end them?*[15]

In the words of Dylan Thomas, We must *"not go gentle into that good night."* Instead, we must, *"Rage, rage against the dying of the light,"* and we must fight for the good things and the great things.

No one ever said reaching destiny and making a difference were easy tasks.

Swimming upstream is never simple, and yet the more one does it, the more natural it becomes. Muscles are developed, new territories are reached, and the joy of fulfilling our potential suffuses our lives.

> No one ever said reaching destiny and making a difference were easy tasks.

In one study of successful people from different walks of life, researchers discovered that the problems high achievers had faced were more severe, not less severe, than those of the average person. One-fourth had major handicaps such as deafness, blindness, or crippled limbs. Three-quarters had come from broken homes or had been born in abject poverty.

The common thread in all their lives was that their problems simply built an even stronger determination to overcome. They chose an attitude of responsibility and learning, refusing to bow down to the victim mentality.

Most people decide not to live purposefully or simply just don't decide at all. The currents of negativity and pressure then invariably sweep their marriage, business, and life downstream to mediocrity or ruin. That is not the way for us. We must have, and hold on to, a different spirit if we are to continue on the road to significance. Upstream is better, not worse, and the benefits of such a life are discovered en route.

I like what the matador once said about the hazards of his profession. *"I'm glad that bulls have horns because, if they didn't, I wouldn't get paid very much!"*

Compare this with the lion tamer who put this advertisement in the paper: *"Lion tamer wants tamer lion!"*

Enduring the Storm

Here then are some practical principles to help you endure in the midst of a storm.

Number One—Realize Storms Never Last

When all is black and destiny seems lost, a shift in the wind can cause things to turn around quickly.

Time itself is a great change agent and healer. What today seems insurmountable and impenetrable can tomorrow be nothing but ruins.

Time itself is a great change agent and healer.

Gandhi's words, which producer Sir Richard Attenborough highlighted in his film about the Indian leader, show how this truth kept Gandhi moving forward toward his destiny:

When I despair, I remember that all through history the way of truth and love has always won. There have been tyrants, and murderers, and for a time they can seem invincible, but in the end they always fall...always.

Shelley, the English poet, is maybe most famous for his poem "Ozymandias," which reminds us how even the mightiest eventually pass away:

I met a traveler from an antique land
Who said:—Two vast and trunkless legs of stone
Stand in the desert. Near them, on the sand,
Half sunk, a shatter'd visage lies, whose frown
And wrinkled lip and sneer of cold command
Tell that its sculptor well those passions read
Which yet survive, stamp'd on these lifeless things,
The hand that mock'd them and the heart that fed.
And on the pedestal these words appear:
"My name is Ozymandias, king of kings:
Look on my works, ye mighty, and despair!"
Nothing beside remains: round the decay
Of that colossal wreck, boundless and bare,
The lone and level sands stretch far away.

Number Two—Resource Yourself

Winston Churchill once said, *"Success is going from failure to failure without loss of enthusiasm."*

The ability to maintain such enthusiasm when all is dark is what divides life's leaders from life's responders. When circumstances in life deplete our energy reserves, we must learn how to resource ourselves. Loss of emotional fuel can and will be fatal on the journey.

> The ability to maintain enthusiasm is what divides life's leaders from life's responders.

Where does this energy come from? I believe there are two major sources:

Friends

Great friends come into their own in the tough times. This is why the value of friendship cannot be overstated. Samuel Johnson put it this way:

To let friendship die away by negligence and silence is certainly not wise. It is voluntarily to throw away one of the greatest comforts of this weary pilgrimage.

In times of trouble a true friend is concerned with helping and challenging, not just commiserating. Now is not the time to have coffee with those who will sympathize and make you feel sorry for yourself. Now is the time to draw strength and encouragement from those who will fan the glowing embers of hope. Remember that a pity party can easily lead to last rites.

A true friend is concerned with helping and challenging, not just commiserating.

The flip side to this coin, however, is that the Super Achiever must have a resource even beyond friends. There are times when we are all alone, totally deserted. If we must have others' input or approval to make it, we will fail.

We will, of course, never have everybody's approval. The realization of this early in life is a major key to forging ahead. It was Bill Cosby who reminded us of the old quote, *"I don't know what the secret of success is, but the secret of failure is trying to please everybody."*

This idea of keeping everybody happy is something that seems to be deeply ingrained within us. Everyone wants to please others by being the types of people others want them to be. There comes a point, however, when such living shows itself to be inauthentic. The result is loss of significance and increase of stress in our lives. This cognitive dissonance begins to erode the very fabric of our souls. At best, we learn to live without fulfilling who we really are. At worst, we become victims, emotionally destroyed and easily manipulated.

Dr. Chris Thurman states,

If you feel that you have to have everyone's approval, I want you to do something that purposely proves you can survive without it. Go yell out the time in the middle of a large store. Walk down the street wearing Mickey Mouse ears. Express a different opinion in a conversation at work tomorrow. If someone asks you to do something that you feel is an unfair request, say no.

I am not encouraging you to do anything unkind, immoral, or dangerous. I am just encouraging you to act in a manner that is consistent with the truth "You can't please everyone."

Oh, and don't be surprised that life will go on, because it will.[16]

Sometimes, then, we persevere with the aid and love of our friends, but we also must be able to continue alone if we desire to follow in the path of the Super Achiever.

There are times when there is no human we can share the anguish with, yet perspective and strength must be obtained. The answer lies, I believe, in connecting with God. In Him, we have the promise of help and peace.

Be anxious for nothing, but in everything by prayer and supplication, with thanksgiving, let your requests be made known to God; and the peace of God, which surpasses all understanding, will guard your hearts and minds through Christ Jesus. (Philippians 4:6–7 NKJV)

The answer lies in connecting with God.

God is always with us. Even more, He has provided a place for us after this life so that we can be with Him for eternity. *"I go to prepare a place for you....I will come again and receive you to Myself; that where I am, there you may be also"* (John 14:2–3 NKJV). Those who put their trust in God gain an eternal perspective because, whatever they must go through on earth, eternity holds the promise of comfort and perfect communion with God.

Supernatural Energy

Throughout history, humanity has realized this hard truth: Loneliness is the companion to pain.

Ella Wheeler Wilcox, in her poem "Solitude," makes this point well:

Laugh, and the world laughs with you;
*   Weep, and you weep alone;*
For the sad old earth must borrow its mirth,
*   But has trouble enough of its own.*
Sing and the hills will answer;
*   Sigh, it is lost on the air;*
The echoes bound to a joyful sound,
*   But shrink from voicing care.*

Rejoice, and men will seek you;
*   Grieve, and they turn and go;*
They want full measure of all your pleasure,

But they do not need your woe.
Be glad, and your friends are many;
Be sad, and you lose them all.
There are none to decline your nectared wine,
But alone you must drink life's gall.

Feast, and your halls are crowded;
Fast, and the world goes by.
Succeed and give, and it helps you live,
But no man can help you die.
There is room in the halls of pleasure;
For a large and lordly train,
But one by one we must all file on
Through the narrow aisles of pain.

Yet all is not lost. The human soul has inner reservoirs of strength that are released when we begin to look beyond ourselves, to our God.

Jesus when He was all alone on the cross; King David when his own troops began to turn on him; Nehemiah when his enemies threatened to tear down the wall at Jerusalem; Job when his family and all his material wealth was taken from him—all relied on God.

> Inner reservoirs of strength are released when we begin to look beyond ourselves.

God desires to be *"a very present help in trouble"* (Psalm 46:1 KJV). Yet we only begin to receive such supernatural help when we come to the end of ourselves and look upward with humility and faith.

This idea of receiving help from God is, for many, like cheating in a game of cards. "Life is tough," they mutter. "We should not be looking for theological morphine to dull the pain of reality."

So, is faith in God merely a crutch for weak minds and cowardly souls, or, on the other hand, is atheism a crutch for those who cannot face the reality of God?

Most people reach the point when it is just them and God.

When one attempts to live without God, the answers to morality, hope, and meaning send one back into his or her own world to fashion an individualized answer. Living without God means lifting oneself up by his or her own metaphysical bootstraps, whichever way is chosen....

Living without God is also making an absolute commitment to a philosophy of life's essence and destiny which, if wrong, affords absolutely no recourse should it be proven false. That is the degree of faith required of one who espouses an antitheistic lifestyle....

Can man live without God? Of course he can, in a physical sense. Can he live without God in a reasonable way? The answer to that is No! because such a person is compelled to deny a moral law, to abandon hope, to forfeit meaning, and to risk no recovery if he is wrong. Life just offers too much evidence to the contrary.[17]

Most people, sometime in life, reach the point when it is just them and God. Well-cemented atheism or fundamentalist pride are quickly dissolved at such moments. Decisions are made within the heart that either reach out a hand to God or shun His beckoning. The choice is ours, and yet, if we turn our backs, the shaft of light, which briefly illuminated our souls, disappears quickly into the fog of our own pride and problems.

Number Three—Hang in There

It is always encouraging to me to learn how many of the world's Super Achievers were average people who simply would not give up or let go of the dream.

We can easily make the mistake of thinking that successful people just get out there and succeed. In reality they just get out there and stay there through failure after failure. The law of percentages slowly begins to work in their favor, and finally the home run is hit, the manuscript is accepted, the business finds its niche, or the vote is won.

Helen Gurley Brown, editor of *Cosmopolitan* for many years, comments that one of the most common mistakes people make in their careers is that they *"check out too soon."* She says they don't want to do the grubby stuff. Instead, they want to reach the top too quickly.

Helen Brown is a good example of the persistence and tenacity required to reach the top. She progressively worked her way up through the organization, giving her best to each job. She calls her willingness to do virtually any job and excel *"mouse burgering"* because, in the beginning, the novice may feel as insignificant as a tiny mouse.

Probably the best encapsulation of this truth is Zig Ziglar's quip, *"The only difference between a big shot and a little shot is that a big shot's just a little shot that kept on shooting."*

It is one thing to have a life purpose, but without this sense of tenacity, dogged determination, and never giving up, a dream can quickly become a fantasy. We enjoy it in our imagination, in the idle moments of life, but we will never see its birth into the real world.

In the final analysis, raw talent is not enough, but simple tenacity will make the difference. From Lincoln to Lindberg, from Franklin to Ford, from Cromwell to Cousteau, the willingness never to give up was the chief aid on the pathway to success. We must learn how to face defeat without being defeated.

Raw talent is not enough, but simple tenacity will make the difference.

Super Achievers have had more than their fair share of disappointments but never live with the regret of giving up. They know how to tough it out, play hurt, grit their teeth, and keep on.

Griessman tells of an interview he had with the legendary singer Ray Charles:

"When the crowd's with you, it does something for you."

"And what do you do," I asked, "when the crowd is small and isn't with you?"

He paused..."That's when you find out whether you're a pro or not....You can't let yourself get down. If you're able to drag on stage, you've gotta be true to thyself. I must be true to Ray."[18]

I personally love the answer actor Bob Hoskins gave when asked about his consistent self-confidence in the face of discouragement and criticism. He said that his mom told him early on, *"Listen, if people don't like you...they've got bad taste."*

Number Four—Remember Your Dream

Remember your dream. Often, as we contemplate the history of our inner revelation of purpose and destiny, the temptation to let go of that purpose will dissipate.

Remembering these key moments of inspiration and direction is fundamental to continuing the journey. Such watersheds in our human experience should be well marked so that we can return to the spot and gain energy for the future.

God ordained that His people build traditions around important milestones for this very reason. The Jewish Passover not only illustrates with powerful symbolism the deliverance from the oppression that the children of Israel suffered, but it also speaks to them anew each year of the unique place they have in the eyes of God and human history.

> Rather than leaving the race, the Super Achiever becomes the servant of a greater destiny.

Tradition, knowledge of history, even nostalgia, can all play parts in moving us forward.

As a minister, when everything within me wants to throw in the towel, I begin to remember my time of calling and, as I do, a gradual strength and assurance begins to build in my heart.

So, when disaster, disappointment, or disability moves in on a Super Achiever, rather than leaving the race, he becomes the servant of a greater destiny—God's purpose for him.

Cripple him, and you have a Sir Walter Scott.

Lock him in a prison cell, and you have a John Bunyan.

Bury him in the snows of Valley Forge, and you have a George Washington.

Raise him in abject poverty, and you have an Abraham Lincoln.

Subject him to bitter religious prejudice, and you have a Disraeli.

Strike him down with infantile paralysis, and he becomes Franklin D. Roosevelt.

Burn him so severely in a schoolhouse fire that the doctors say he will never walk again, and you have a Glenn Cunningham, who set the world's record in 1934 for running a mile in 4 minutes and 6.7 seconds.

Deafen a genius composer, and you have a Ludwig van Beethoven.

Have him or her born black in a society filled with racial discrimination, and you have a Booker T. Washington, a Harriet Tubman, a Marian Anderson, a George Washington Carver, or a Martin Luther King, Jr....

Call him a slow learner, "retarded," and write him off as uneducable, and you have an Albert Einstein.[19]

No excuses. No victims. No crybabies. No nonsense. No paranoia!

The world is not plotting against us, but life is tough. Problems and pain exist, but they must never be allowed to conquer the soul.

The indomitable heart of the Super Achiever marches on....

IN PRAISE OF SUPER ACHIEVERS
Abundance Mentality

"A man who isn't a socialist at 20 has no heart, and a man who is a socialist at 40 has no head."

Aristide Briand

Chapter Seven

In Praise of Super Achievers

There are many on the ladder of success who believe that, in order to get to the top, they have to dislodge those above them and tread on those beneath them. Success, however, is not a ladder; it is a journey along a road on which we can all travel. The travelers upon this road, if they really want to get to the destination, are better off helping their fellow travelers, not attacking them.

Super Achievers do not operate with an "I win, you lose" mentality but with an "I win, you win" idea of life. This is initially surprising for, when people begin to study the lives of Super Achievers, they probably expect to find individuals who are highly competitive and fight to win at all costs. Interestingly, this type of attitude is a rarity.

Super Achievers understand that individual success does not necessarily mean the failure of others. They have what I term an "abundance mentality." They want to succeed, they want to do well, they want to reach their goals, and they are not in any way hampered by feelings of guilt. Guilt only accompanies those who think in terms of, "I win, you lose."

The scarcity mentality sees the economic world as a kind of pie with only so many pieces to go around. The more I get on my plate, the less for everyone else. If one considers this to be a good thing, he becomes confrontational and competitive. If one considers this to be a bad thing, he becomes unmotivated and guilty of success. In an effort to appease conscience, many lower their standards and settle for mediocrity.

Success does not just occur naturally and spontaneously.

The truth is, life is not like a pie. My receiving more does not mean everyone else receives less. Conrad Black, the Canadian media baron, puts it this way:

> It is a myth of the left and one of the well-springs of the pervasive...spirit of envy that the success of a person implies the failure or exploitation of someone else. Our economic system is not based on single-combat war or a zero-sum game.

I cannot, as a believer in a good God, accept that the system for advancement He created has been designed with this inevitable, win-lose paradigm. The notion that one person's gain must be another's loss simply does not gel, and it is contradicted by the concepts of service, giving, team, and family.

On the other hand, success does not just occur naturally and spontaneously. Paul Zane Pilzer elaborates on this point:

> God, our Father, did not put us on earth to profit at the expense of one another. Implicit within this belief is our understanding that, like a loving father, God would not simply hand over to us, his children, everything that we desired. Rather, he would give us the tools that we

require to succeed, and allow us to discover for ourselves how to use them.[20]

There is plenty for everyone. The pie analogy only works, thinking of it in purely economic terms, if we give to the pie the possibility of expansion. Creativity, entrepreneurship, and individual effort cause such growth.

All our lives, most of us have been subjected to an economic model based on scarcity theory. We have been told there is a limit to the amount of available wealth. This traditional view has forgotten the element of human ingenuity, which constantly redefines what has value and what does not.

Paul Zane Pilzer explains this in his historical overview of valued resources. He points out that, in the nineteenth century, the supply of whale blubber shrank, so we found a way to make use of the "worthless" black goo that oozed from the ground in Texas. And today, the most important technology, the microchip, is made out of the most common material—sand.[21]

Population may have increased, but gross world product also continues to increase, and at a much higher and exponential rate. Not only is progress continuing, but the progress of progress as well.

This simply means that the average worker's buying power, per hour of work, is steadily increasing. The concept of unlimited wealth is a point that has been vigorously debated in economic circles. It even prompted a bet between Julian Simon (author of *The Ultimate Resource*, which argues that people are "the ultimate" resource) and Paul Ehrlich, hero of the gloom and doom set.

In 1980, Simon issued the challenge, betting that the price of any natural resource at any future date would be reduced. Ehrlich accepted, and the bet was formalized in October 1980.

The combined prices of five metals—chrome, copper, nickel, tin, and tungsten—were chosen. Should the price rise, Ehrlich would win. If it dropped, Simon would collect. Ten years later, the bet was settled with Simon victorious. The price for the metals had fallen to 57.6 percent of the 1980 price. If we include the effect of inflation, the price was as low as 30 percent of the 1980 figure.[22]

Wealth is not limited to physical resource but to human creativity. The nation of Singapore is a good example of this. Over the last forty years, without the necessary raw materials, physical space, or rich, arable farmland, this country has grown its economy considerably. Its people simply added initiative, dreams, entrepreneurship, wisdom, and persistence to the picture.

> Wealth is not limited to physical resource but to human creativity.

A person only has to talk to those brought up with a background of socialism, or one of its kindred philosophies, to understand that the dream of egalitarianism is never realized. When we continue to penalize those who achieve in life and subsidize those who refuse to take initiative, we are failing—failing to understand that helping and rewarding the achiever causes resources, expertise, and all their ancillary benefits to flow down to everybody in society.

Bureaucratic red tape that continually tries to level the playing field can often dissipate the very qualities that are necessary for the success of a society.

When faith dies, so does enterprise. It is impossible to create a system of collective regulation and safety that does not finally deaden the moral sources of the willingness to face danger and fight, that does not dampen the spontaneous flow of gifts and experiments which extend the dimensions of the world and the circles of human sympathy.

The ultimate strength and crucial weakness of both capitalism and democracy are their reliance on individual creativity and courage, leadership and morality, intuition and faith. But there is no alternative, except mediocrity and stagnation....

Certain knowledge, to the extent that it ever comes, is given us only after the moment of opportunity has passed. The venturer who awaits the emergence of a safe market, the tax-cutter who demands full assurance of new revenue, the leader who seeks a settled public opinion, all will always act too timidly and too late.[23]

Capitalism, when married to a strong moral framework and values base that includes philanthropy, duty, and faith, should result in the rich *and* the poor getting richer. Surely the truth is that if the rich are not getting richer, they are doing something wrong. To be wise and proactive when one already has resources to work with should create more wealth and, as a result, benefit rather than harm society. So then, Super Achievers realize that their success is God's way of helping other people.

> If the rich are not getting richer, they are doing something wrong.

While it may be true that the gap between rich and poor is growing, it should also be true that the poor are doing better as well. The best way to help a society is to encourage those with money to use it, invest it, spend it, and give it. This will create a growing economy, increased employment, and more opportunities.

The best way to help a society is to encourage those with money to use it.

George Gilder, in his book *Wealth and Poverty*, produces a lengthy and compelling argument for what he calls *"supply side economics."* He shows that there is nothing wrong with those who are well-off shouldering more responsibility for the well-being of their society. This is often reflected in graduated tax rates. However, when the rate approaches or surpasses 50 percent, the revenue received by government actually begins to decrease. This is simply the result of those at this level beginning to work much harder at minimizing their tax. Add to this the dwindling incentive for earning more money, and one begins to see the practical truth of Gilder's position.

The Laffer curve reveals this theory in a simple way. Economist Arthur Laffer realized that there are probably two different tax rates that will produce a similar amount of revenue. For example, a zero rate will bring in no revenue, and a 100 percent rate will also result in nothing because it would put a stop to taxable enterprise. Lower tax rates stimulate business and move capital into taxable activity, thus increasing revenue for government. Achievers again begin to achieve, cash flow throughout society is increased, employment rises, and projects designed to help the needy and those dependent upon society are better resourced.

Bountiful Eyes

Super Achievers are never threatened by someone else's success. They do not allow jealousy or greed to dominate their thinking processes. They understand the wisdom of Proverbs when it says, *"He that hath a bountiful eye shall be blessed"* (Proverbs 22:9 KJV). We must realize that our own success should help others, not hinder them. When this truth is understood, we will begin to move out of the fog of self-interest and the destructive style of confrontational competition and into the clear light of freedom and achievement.

The Super Achiever next door should inspire us to grow and achieve, not make us jealous. To cut achievers down is to join the throng of those who believe that mediocrity is normal and that color, vibrancy, and dreaming are somehow culpable for the ills of society. Those who would rather live in that gray, formless world shun challenge and risk taking. That is no way for the Super Achiever to live.

MY BRAIN HURTS
Constant Learning

"Anyone who stops learning is old, whether at twenty or eighty. Anyone who keeps learning stays young."

Henry Ford

Chapter Eight

My Brain Hurts

The quest for knowledge, insight, and wisdom is part and parcel of the life of the one who excels. The reason for this is self-evident. Super Achievers realize that, as the circle of knowledge grows, so also does the boundary of ignorance. Or, to put it another way, the more we learn, the more we realize how much we don't know. This revelation of what we don't know will continue to motivate us toward learning.

> ## The more we learn, the more we realize how much we don't know.

There are many things in life that I know. I know how to drive a car. I know how to speak English. I know how to make béarnaise sauce (although the right application of that knowledge evades me more often than not!). Alternatively, there are many things I don't know. I don't know how to speak Chinese. I don't know how to navigate the Amazon. I don't know how to make an igloo.

There are other things that I not only know, but I also know that I know them; things I have a certain and absolute knowledge of. I know that I know that my name is Phil Baker. I know that I know that I live in Australia.

Then there are many things that I don't know, but I know that I don't know them. I don't know how to be a handyman around the house. I don't know how to fix a car if it breaks down. However, I have an advantage over many other men in that, although I don't know these things, I know that I don't know them! Therefore, I don't attempt to fix the car or mend the broken gate, much to the relief of my wife! She is happy because, when things are broken, we get a suitably qualified person to come, and whatever is broken is fixed professionally. The few times I tried to dabble in this area, disaster was almost always the result.

A little while ago, we blew a fuse in our house. Being the gallant man of the family, and having just watched an episode of *Home Improvement,* I declared to my wife and children, "No problem. Father is here!" I went out to the fuse box and tried to remove the faulty fuse. I discovered it was jammed in its socket, so I took a screwdriver and began to pry it loose. My heroic act quickly ended when a belt of electricity knocked me over. Concurrent with the surge of power, there was a flash of insight that told me I had forgotten to turn the main switch off. So, as you can see, I have an amazing capacity to make a mess of home-repair tasks, even simple ones like changing a fuse. Thus you can understand my family's joy when I declare that I know that I don't know about such matters.

> As the circle of knowledge grows, so does the boundary of ignorance.

Where is all this leading us? Well, if there are things that I know and things that I don't know; things that I know that I know and things that I know that I don't know—think how many things there must be that I don't know and don't even know that I don't know them!

I am happily enjoying my life, doing what I am called to do, and yet there are a multitude of things concerning what I do that I don't know about, and I don't even know that I don't know them. This revelation alone will cause me to be a continual learner. Maybe today—in a seminar, reading a book, in a relationship, during a conversation—I might learn something that I didn't know, which will enable me to be more effective in the journey that lies ahead.

Super Achievers are always reading, listening to others, and seeking advice. The book of Proverbs puts it this way: *"The wise in heart will receive commandments: but a prating fool shall fall....Wise men lay up knowledge: but the mouth of the foolish is near destruction"* (Proverbs 10:8, 14 KJV). The biblical fool is not one whose IQ is deficient but one whose attitude toward life is that of non-absorption and refusal to listen.

Art Buchwald, one of America's greatest humorists, put it this way:

> *There are too many people who think they're educated because they have a diploma....They aren't. You don't get educated; you prepare yourself for an education. You prepare yourself to know how to look things up, to know how to use books, how to think.*

The love of learning and the love of books are common traits for Super Achievers. Truman was a constant reader, as was Kennedy. The latter's reading of history was a key to his decision-making process during the Cuban Missile Crisis.

Kennedy had been reading Barbara Tuchman's history of World War I, *The Guns of August*. He was amazed at how the beginning of the war could have been avoided. Over-reaction, prejudices, personality clashes...he was determined that the same mistakes would not be made in what could have become World War III.

The importance of input cannot be overstated. Our thinking has a direct connection to our actions. To change how we behave, we must change how we think. Therefore, solid nutritional brain food is essential.

> Learning must be accompanied by the willingness to listen to others.

As Griessman writes, *"High achievers may attain breadth of knowledge, but they always obtain depth of knowledge in some one area. They may know a little about a lot of things, but they always know a lot about one thing."*

Mental breadth and depth are expanded as we take in sound information and give ourselves to purposeful contemplation. Blaise Pascal, my favorite philosopher, put it this way: *"Man's greatness lies in his power of thought."*

The arrogance of youth, which refuses to ask questions, has destroyed many a life. Those who wish to get ahead must pursue those who have already gotten there and pick their brains for answers, ideas, and perspectives on life. In this sense, one could rightly call Super Achievers humble people in that they never think they know it all and are always open to the advice and input of those around them.

Remaining objective is the key. Great learning must be accompanied by the willingness to listen to others. This is an important point and should not be glossed over. The tragedy of the intellectual is all too often the incipient and slow-creeping arrogance that blinds the mind and limits the boundaries of growth. We can get too clever for our own good and, by looking for the intricate, miss the elegance and simplicity of truth.

G. K. Chesterton makes this point well:

Now, one of these four or five paradoxes which should be taught to every infant prattling at his mother's knee is the following: that the more a man looks at a thing, the less he can see it, and the more a man learns a thing the less he knows it. The Fabian argument of the expert, that the man who is trained should be the man who is trusted, would be absolutely unanswerable if it were really true that a man who studied a thing and practiced it every day went on seeing more and more of its significance. But he does not. He goes on seeing less and less of its significance.[24]

We must realize that to reach our goals we will need as much help as we can get. We should not confuse the getting of information with its application—with wisdom. The achiever asks penetrating questions that yield practical results on the road to destiny. These continual reality checks, helicoptering up to see the big picture, are key in keeping us on track.

Input Is Vital

The realization that input is vital for success—that right input leads to right results—carries with it a natural corollary. Wrong input will lead to wrong results. What we feed on as individuals will affect our thinking, then our beliefs, and finally our actions. In this information age, when the chatter in cyberspace can be deafening, it is important to screen what we allow into our hearts and minds.

Super Achievers realize that a constant diet of garbage, misinformation, and negativity could derail them on the journey toward their life goals. The habit of continual learning must be accompanied by a continual sifting through of the available informational resources in such a way as to ponder and study only those things that inspire, challenge, and lead to growth and health.

> Our society today seems to have mistaken quantity of information for quality.

Unfortunately, our society today seems to have mistaken quantity of information for quality. Our press is filled with gossip rather than news. Our churches feed us dos and don'ts rather than the blessings God has promised. Our relationships are often draining rather than replenishing. And our televisions are filled with what Frank Lloyd Wright called *"Chewing gum for the mind."* Chewing gum is good in its own place, but a constant diet of it will lead to malnourishment and loss of energy.

Rousseau once said that truth is to be sought, not in the ideas and behavior of corrupt dwellers of sophisticated cities, but in the pure heart of a simple peasant or innocent child, where it is more likely to be found. Our lives are surrounded by, and revolve around, trivia. There simply is no time and no example to point us elsewhere.

Sport scores interest us more than sunsets. Our eyes are on the detail, and the picture eludes us. We are too busy watching *Friends* on television to be friends in life. We are like photographers on a wedding day, so intent on our task of capturing the moments that, to us, the photo becomes more real than the life it portrays. One wonders if tourists would see more and live more if they were not continually looking through the lens. Life is not a dress rehearsal. We must stop now and then to look and ponder.

In Praise of Thinking

Most people think only once or twice in their lifetime. The reason I have been so successful is that I have been able to think once or twice a year. —Victor Hugo

Our brains are amazing pieces of equipment, able to process thirty billion bits of information at once while utilizing the equivalent of six thousand miles of wiring and cabling. Yet this neural network can sit mostly dormant for a lifetime.

We must learn how to think. We must educate our children in a way that trains them to reason and discern, not just do.

We must learn how to think.

The problem with outcome or vocational education theory is that it produces capable workers who are unable to operate successfully outside the narrow parameters of job descriptions.

Employers lament the lack of thinkers graduating from our major institutions. I am not talking here about IQ but about the creative, imaginative breadth of knowledge-type people, who are more than simply processors of information.

The push to remove art subjects—English, philosophy, history, and the like—from our curricula is the chief culprit for this loss of enquiring minds. Sir Robert Jones, for many years New Zealand's leading real estate entrepreneur, is just one of the growing number of frustrated employers.

He tells of a management conference his company conducted for its top managerial trainees. The subject under discussion was techniques for leasing vacant space in a weak market. Jones pointed out to the trainees that in more competitive foreign markets, the practice was to put signs on buildings. This traditionally had not been done in New Zealand because the signs spoiled the buildings' appearance and, until recently, it was relatively easy to lease space without taking such measures.

"Should we now adopt this practice?" I asked.

There followed a generally inane discussion, so I narrowed the issue and put the proposition, "Why do you suppose other nations continue doing this year after year?" Someone pitifully suggested because it might be considered good advertising for the real estate company. The others sat in stupefying silence. The obvious answer "because it works," was totally beyond those heavily university-degreed minds.

These people are not stupid...but they can't think. They have gone straight from college and acquired their law and commerce degrees and missed out on an education. Sadly, what we are finding in our company is that many of our best thinkers have never been near a university.[25]

The fault is partly with the employers as well. It is easy in this technical world to hire people based on grades and diplomas without placing value on the benefits of a classical education.

It has been humorously observed that a graduate with a science degree asks, "Why does it work?" The graduate with an engineering degree asks, "How does it work?" The graduate with an accounting degree asks, "How much will it cost?" The graduate with an arts degree asks, "Do you want fries with that?"

Times, however, are changing. People are beginning to realize the importance of ideas and the power of the individual thinking process.

Ed Cole observed that the person without an organized system of thought is always at the mercy of the person who has one. Thus we must strive to develop this crucial area of our lives, both in the continual getting of information and in the discipline of imaginative and creative thought.

The heart and mind of the Super Achiever requires jet fuel, not watered-down diesel, to reach her life goal. We must listen to big people and immerse ourselves in the big ideas of our world. There simply is not enough time for superficial, pedantic, or banal things to dominate our cognitive abilities. We need inspiration, not just information. We need courage, not cowardice. We need passion, not pettiness. We will discover ourselves with solitude and searching, not superstitions and soap operas. We will finally reach our destination with discipline and deep thinking, not dalliance and diversion.

LIFESTYLES OF THE RICH AND MISERABLE

Contentment

"I want to be what I was when I wanted to be what I am now."

Graffiti, London 1980

Chapter Nine

Lifestyles of the Rich and Miserable

Out of all the qualities we have looked at, contentment seems to be the most elusive. The truth of the inside-out philosophy is easily drowned out by the many voices of materialism.

To be honest, for our generation, there is more to have—much more. Jesus pointed out that real life does not consist in the abundance of possessions, yet surely this is not true for us. I mean, after all, now we have our automatic locks and our espresso machines, wide-screen TVs and designer dogs. Magazines such as *Robb Report* devote themselves to showing us what is available. They repeatedly tell us that we would be more fulfilled and contented if only we had some new product or a deluxe vacation. The only trouble is that, after the Learjets and the limousines have been flown and driven, the "if only" remains.

The more we have, the more we want. External wealth often produces internal craving, and so the cycle repeats itself.

The winter of our discontent progressively gets colder and drearier. It deadens joy, removes wonder, and reduces life to just survival.

Constant craving for what is not robs us of the ability to enjoy and celebrate what is. In Shakespeare's words from *King Lear,* "Striving to better, oft we mar what's well."

I used to be happy with flying—the takeoff, the movie, the view. Happy, that is, until I had the opportunity of flying first class between Sydney and Los Angeles.

A friend had arranged a special ticket for almost the same price as coach class, so I jumped at my chance to experience life at the front of the plane. Upon check-in, I began to notice the differences. I was called, "Mr. Baker," and "Sir," instead of the normal, "Ticket please," and "No, all the aisle seats are occupied." I was taken to a special lounge and enjoyed the chardonnay and the Camembert. Then they began boarding. All those other people got on first so that, when we were asked to join the flight, there were no lines or noise. Just classical music, French champagne, and seats that actually were seats!

> Constant craving for what is not robs us of the ability to enjoy what is.

The personal video screen, complete with sports, documentaries, and all the latest movies, was my next discovery, but nothing could prepare me for dinner. Up to this point in time, the phrase "airline food" was an oxymoron, much like "council worker." How quickly that concept changed.

Beluga Caviar

"Would you like Russian vodka with that, Sir?"

Fillet steak, medium rare, with fresh asparagus.

"Béarnaise sauce, Sir?"

Chocolate parfait, international cheeseboard, and a choice of Chateau d'Yquem, vintage port, or brewed coffee.

"Or would you like all three, Sir?"

Later on during the flight, after my second movie, I decided to venture out of my stress-free environment. Call it nostalgia, call it gloating, but I was going to go through the curtain.

The first stage of my walk was through business class. Seats slightly smaller, occupants slightly more ambitious. I felt their grudging respect, as I was one of the few passengers that were better off than they. The second curtain loomed before me. British Airways calls their business class Club World. First class is referred to as Fantasy World. I was, however, about to step into Third World. The scene that confronted me was all too familiar: People trying to sleep in positions they could not normally hold for more than a few minutes; babies crying; lines at the bathrooms; an entire rugby team calling for another round. I beat a hasty retreat to the safety and security of life at the front.

Contentment is the holy grail everyone seems to be searching for.

This whole experience has taught me several things. First of all, I am a first-class citizen. I belong there. I desire to be there. I need to be there! Second, it taught me that the upgrade is worth both bribery and begging. (Free copies of this book are available to any airline personnel who have this coveted power of granting the upgrade!) Third, I have discovered that now I don't enjoy flying. No longer am I content in my economy seat. I know what lies beyond the curtain!

Contentment is the holy grail everyone seems to be searching for. Money, respect, pleasure, and success are merely the chosen roads that travelers hope reach this destination. Yet, as Ravi Zacharias points out, contentment remains elusive for many:

> One of the most common refrains we hear from those who have reached the pinnacle of success is that of the emptiness that still stalks their lives, all their successes notwithstanding. That sort of confession is at least one reason the question of meaning is so central to life's pursuit. Although none like to admit it, what brings purpose in life for many, particularly in countries rich in enterprising opportunities, is a higher standard of living, even if it means being willing to die for it. Yet, judging by the remarks of some who have attained those higher standards, there is frequently an admission of disappointment.[26]

Zacharias then proceeds to give some examples:

> After his second Wimbledon victory, Boris Becker surprised the world by admitting his great struggle with suicide. Jack Higgins, the renowned author of The Eagle Has Landed, has said that the one thing he knows now at this high point of his career that he wished he had known as a small boy is this: "When you get to the top, there's nothing there."[27]

To this, could be added the words of Lee Iacocca, chairman of Chrysler:

> Here I am in the twilight years of my life, still wondering what it's all about....I can tell you this, fame and fortune is for the birds.

He goes on to explain that, for him, it was only family and close friends that brought the contentment that he so deeply desired.

John Gatto, New York's Teacher of the Year from 1989–1991, lamented the impact of materialistic thinking on young people:

> *These things are killing us as a nation: narcotic drugs, brainless competition, recreational sex, the pornography of violence, gambling, alcohol, and the worst pornography of all—lives devoted to buying things, accumulation as a philosophy. All of them are addictions of dependent personalities.*

For many, contentment is tied up with what we have and how much we earn, yet study after study reveals that satisfaction isn't so much getting what you want but wanting what you have.

In other words, there are two ways to be rich. One is to have great wealth. The other is to have few wants. David Myers, in his book *The Pursuit of Happiness*, recounts how this truth was observed by a former nurse in a Nigerian village:

> Satisfaction isn't so much getting what you want but wanting what you have.

> *A group of five- to seven-year-old boys wearing rags for clothes were racing along our compound's driveway with a toy truck made of tin cans from my trash. They had spent the greater part of the morning engineering their toy—and were squealing with delight as they pushed it with a stick. My sons, with Tonka trucks parked under their beds, looked on with envy.*[28]

One has only to watch the family dynamic of children playing with their parents on a street in Calcutta. Compare this with the formal, restless, and busy existence of most of the Western world's middle-class homes, and we quickly realize that there is more to life than simply cash flow.

Making more money does not increase happiness. Being rich is something we have or don't have within us.

Thomas Ludwig, together with David Myers, in studying the money/happiness question, revealed how we create our own discontent when we describe our inability to buy everything as poverty. Such "poor talk" (grumbling about the price of milk and bread on the way to and from the store in our new four-wheel-drive vehicle) is highly objectionable. We need to be more honest and admit that, when spending outstrips income, the problem is lack of discipline or priorities, not that we are unable to afford life's necessities.

Making more money does not increase happiness.

Such talk is not only offensive to those who are truly poor, but it also pollutes our thinking and magnifies our discontent. We begin to believe our own propaganda and reduce ourselves to self-pitying victims who are whining about what two-thirds of the world's population would rejoice over. Thus we need to change our vocabulary. As Myers writes,

"I need that" can become "I want that." "I am underpaid" can become, "I spend more than I make." And that most familiar middle-class lament, "We can't afford it!" can become, more truthfully, "We choose to spend our money on other things." For usually we could

afford it...if we made it our top priority; we just have other priorities on which we choose to spend our limited incomes.[29]

Jesus, speaking to His disciples, told them not to worry about material things, saying, *"Life is more than food, and the body more than clothes"* (Luke 12:23 NIV). He then went on to explain that if they would seek Him rather than the world and material goods, He would provide for all their needs:

> *Consider the ravens: They do not sow or reap, they have no storeroom or barn; yet God feeds them. And how much more valuable you are than birds!...Consider how the lilies grow. They do not labor or spin. Yet I tell you, not even Solomon in all his splendor was dressed like one of these. If that is how God clothes the grass of the field, which is here today, and tomorrow is thrown into the fire, how much more will he clothe you, O you of little faith! And do not set your heart on what you will eat or drink; do not worry about it. For the pagan world runs after all such things, and your Father knows that you need them. But seek his kingdom, and these things will be given to you as well.* (Luke 12:24, 27–31 NIV)

Contentment

So what is this secret art of contentment? I believe that, as we all begin to practice the habits and cultivate the attitude of the Super Achiever, we will learn the truth of inward contentment. Such things as an overriding goal, focus, self-growth, and humility all are prerequisites for internal harmony.

The lesson must be learned that contentment is not necessarily to be found in the palaces of the super-rich or around the boardroom tables of business tycoons but in the trusting, God-fearing, and self-giving hearts of average people.

In looking back over my life, I would have to say that, when happiness and contentment levels were the highest, my external circumstances—house and income—were often at their lowest.

Discerning what is more is easy; discerning what is better is hard.

I can remember playing with my sister when I was a child in a tiny back garden of a semidetached house in a suburb of the Medway towns. We had hours of fun playing with a tire that swung from the only vegetation in the garden, a small stunted and battered tree.

A year later, after emigrating from England to New Zealand, we found ourselves living on a small farm by a beautiful river mouth in the subtropical North. We had oceanfront and riverfront property. Fishing, surfing, canoeing, and horseback riding were all available to us, and yet it seems to me that life was more fun swinging from the tire. As David Myers said, *"The river of happiness is fed far less by wealth than by the streams of ordinary pleasures."*

In the final analysis, what we think is superior often disappoints. Discerning what is more is easy; discerning what is better is hard.

"What keeps our faith cheerful," says Garrison Keillor, *"is everywhere in daily life, a sign that faith rules through*

ordinary things: through cooking and small talk, through story telling, making love, fishing, tending animals and sweet corn and flowers, through sports, music, and books, raising kids—all the places where the gravy soaks in and grace shines through. Even in a time of elephantine vanity and greed, one never has to look far to see the campfires of gentle [and happy] people."[30]

FLYING WITH THE DUCKS

People Believers

"Coming together is a beginning, staying together is progress, and working together is success."

Henry Ford

Chapter Ten

Flying with the Ducks

There
is something about a great woman or man that radiates outward into the lives of those around them. This radiation is not just a natural occurrence; it is the result of a purposeful belief in people. Super Achievers see the people around them from the perspective of their potential, rather than their actual behavior. They are slow to carry a grudge and quick to forgive. They encourage, inspire, and cause their friends, employees, and coworkers to grow larger on the inside. Very rarely do you find a Super Achiever who goes it alone.

Super Achievers see the people around them from the perspective of their potential.

More and more, great leaders of our day find the best way to work is to work through people, to build teams, and to develop synergy.

This idea of synergy is an integral value in the lives of Super Achievers. They honestly evaluate their own weaknesses and call others alongside who have abilities in those areas. They have an ability to draw on the strength of others and, as a result, become more effective and efficient in the journey toward their life goals.

To my mind, the concept of synergy has best been described, in the words of Zig Ziglar, as a group of ducks flying. If you have ever observed ducks (or similar migrating birds) in flight, you will immediately notice two things. First, they always fly in a V formation. Second, one side of the V is always slightly longer than the other side. The reason for both observations is highly significant. For one, the reason that one side of the V is always slightly longer is simply because the side that is longer has more ducks in it!

On a more serious note, the reason ducks fly in a V formation is to take advantage of the partial wind vacuum created in the wake of each duck. By periodically changing the lead duck, they can fly nearly twice as far together as they could on their own.

This team truth is, I believe, self-evident. Not only is it the most effective way of getting things done, but it is also the most fun.

Sports history is replete with examples of a team of average players defeating a group of gifted individuals. A great music group is not so much about the brilliance of a solo act any of the musicians may bring to the table but about how well they play together. Even in the dog-eat-dog world of business, this teamwork idea has resulted in a paradigm shift, as evidenced by the number of business books released in recent years with the word *team* included in the title.

Super Achievers know that through tenacity, persistence, hard work, motivation, goal setting, vision, and discipline they will go a long way. However, if they can harness the energy, talents, and dreams of the people around them, helping one another fulfill their destinies in life, then all the team members will excel, and the results will be exponentially greater. The Bible puts it this way: *"One chase a thousand, and two put ten thousand to flight"* (Deuteronomy 32:30 KJV). However, one reason many people fail to achieve in life is simply that they find it very difficult to trust other people.

We judge based on who we are. Trustworthy people are themselves trusting. Believing in others to the point of naive optimism often indicates sound character. Their idealistic views about others are based on how they operate as individuals. This is why the one who is of doubtful character or criminal intent cannot trust other people to be honest. He

> The willingness to be hurt enables us to experience the joy of relationships.

knows himself too well and assumes that everyone is just like him.

A latent cynicism and mistrust in people will strike at the roots of significance every time. That is why Jesus' words about loving one another are so important.

> *Love one another. As I have loved you, so you must love one another. By this all men will know that you are my disciples, if you love one another.* (John 13:34–35 NIV)

We must refuse to allow hurts, insults, or injuries we've received to dissolve our optimism and faith in humanity. To fail here is to limit our own hearts and therefore our lives' progression. The glass ceiling of past hurt and bitterness is a primary reason for the loss of fulfilled destiny. First Peter 4:8 says, *"Love each other deeply, because love covers over a multitude of sins"* (NIV).

The willingness to be hurt enables us to experience the joy of relationships. Pain, coupled with joy, is what life is all about.

This simple yet profound point has best been brought out in, of all things, a children's story about a much-loved but battered toy:

> The Skin Horse had lived longer in the nursery than any of the others. He was so old that his brown coat was bald in patches and showed the seams underneath, and most of the hairs in his tail had been pulled out to string bead necklaces. He was wise, for he had seen a long succession of mechanical toys arrive to boast and swagger, and by-and-by break their mainsprings and pass away, and he knew that they were only toys, and would never turn into anything else. For nursery magic is very strange and wonderful, and only those playthings that are old and wise and experienced like the Skin Horse understand all about it.
>
> "What is REAL?" asked the Rabbit one day, when they were lying side by side near the nursery fender, before Nana came to tidy the room. "Does it mean having things that buzz inside you and a stick-out handle?"
>
> "Real isn't how you are made," said the Skin Horse. "It's a thing that happens to you. When a child loves you for a long, long time, not just to play with, but REALLY loves you, then you become real."
>
> "Does it hurt?" asked the Rabbit.
>
> "Sometimes," said the Skin Horse, for he was always truthful. "When you are Real you don't mind being hurt."
>
> "Does it happen all at once, like being wound up," he asked, "or bit by bit?"
>
> "It doesn't happen all at once," said the Skin Horse. "You become. It takes a long time. That's why it doesn't

often happen to people who break easily, or have sharp edges, or who have to be carefully kept. Generally, by the time you are Real, most of your hair has been loved off, and your eyes drop out and you get loose in the joints and very shabby. But these things don't matter at all, because once you are real you can't be ugly, except to people who don't understand."[31]

It is when we love and are loved, believe in others and sense their faith in us as well, that we discover what it is to become truly human. We cannot survive as simply autonomous units. This is the truth of community, of family, and of friendship. We are part of one another. To disengage is to die. John Donne embedded this in our hearts and minds when he wrote, *"No man is an island, entire of itself; every man is a piece of the continent, a part of the main."*

To reach a goal on one's own is often a hollow and lonely experience. To bring a team, family, or a group of friends together and see the dream realized corporately brings community to success and success to community. In the final analysis we all need, in the words of Joe Cocker at Woodstock, *"a little help from our friends."*

KEEPING OUT OF THE DITCHES
Balance

"Moderation is a fatal thing. Nothing succeeds like excess."

Oscar Wilde

Chapter Eleven

Keeping out of the Ditches

Most of us like to think of ourselves as well balanced. The concept of balance, however, is highly subjective. One person's moderation is another person's extreme. One person's floor is another person's ceiling. Yet I firmly believe that there is a middle of the road, and progress toward destiny is far more effective when our wheels are firmly on the asphalt rather than off on the shoulder.

Balance is, of course, not an equal amount of opposites. The half-good, half-evil person or the answer that is half-right and half-wrong is not what we are talking about. I am also not referring to the person who believes his relational equilibrium is in order simply because he has a chip on each shoulder.

Achieving balance is no small feat. We tend toward the edges. Call it curiosity, call it adolescence, call it stupidity; but most of us, for most of the time, drive with a couple of wheels on the shoulder. We are this way individually, and we are this way as communities and nations.

Pascal highlighted this idea:

What a chimera, then, is a man! what a novelty, what a monster, what a chaos, what a subject of contradiction, what a prodigy! A judge of all things, feeble worm of the earth, depository of truth, a cloaca of uncertainty and error, the glory and the shame of the universe.[32]

Why is it that we have this potential? Why couldn't God have created humankind out of better stuff? C. S. Lewis pointed out that the better the stuff something is made of, the greater the potential for either extreme. A cow can be neither good nor bad. A child, of course, can be. An adult can be either very good or very evil. A genius can be the best or the worst of all.

Balance is a rare commodity.

Balance, then, whether we are talking about the individual life or the whole nation, is a rare commodity. The question is, Does balance tend toward achievement, or is the balanced individual handicapped when it comes to the race toward destiny?

When I first began to study this important area of reaching goals and fulfilling dreams, I believed that extremists would have the edge. Those who are prepared to sacrifice everything on the altar of their passion stood a better chance than those who were more balanced and whole. I immediately thought of some people who had achieved great things; people who were highly eccentric and totally obsessed; people who had achieved greatness at the expense of family, friends, and their own health. However, as I studied further, I began to realize that this supposition was way off the mark.

True success cannot be relegated to one division of life. A person who succeeds in business but fails in her personal relational world and dies early of a work-induced heart attack can hardly be called successful. Wholesomeness, health, and success in every area of life are generally not found in those who are extreme. The Super Achiever is not found amongst religious fanatics, food bingers, TV addicts, or fasting martyrs. Success must be seen holistically; it is the result of effective management of life and priorities, as well as the ability to keep perspective. Those who excel in life usually have a strong faith in God, commitment to family, and a sense of values that causes them to live by conviction rather than by preference.

This whole book is about the necessity of balance between inner and outer; that among our lattes and laptops, our salads and cell phones, we give thought to the soul.

Alarmingly, simple technological progress, despite its ability to make life more convenient, creates as many problems as it solves. As one writer states,

> We did not know acid rain would result from burning fossil fuels. We did not know mobility would disrupt family and community stability. We did not know inner city housing projects would turn into ghetto war zones. We did not know thalidomide would deform babies. We did not invent suburbs to throw our traffic patterns into chaos.[33]

Progress has magnified our flaws and given us greater opportunity for self-destruction. Richard Swenson makes this point well:

> We have put armaments in the hands of our hostility, litigation in the hands of our cynicism, affluence in the hands of our greed, the media in the hands of our decadence, advertisements in the hands of our discontent, pornography in the hands of our lust and education in the hands of our pride.[34]

We are able to live faster, but we die quicker, if not on the outside, then certainly on the inside. To use Solzenhitsyn's words, *"We are in an insane, ill-considered, furious dash into a blind alley."*

Strengths and Weaknesses

It is an interesting point to note, at this juncture, that balance does not mean equal competence in all departments of life.

We all have strengths and weaknesses. There are some traits we excel in and others we spend our whole lives working on simply to get to the point where they are not a hindrance. It would be wrong to assume that a Super Achiever is one who has equal mastery over all the characteristics covered in this book. They may have a handle on the majority of them, but no one is omni-competent.

> Balance is about maximizing our strengths while working on our weaknesses.

Most prime ministers and presidents are voted in on their strengths and lose on their weaknesses. Nixon was appointed because of his strong directional, take-no-prisoners type of leadership, but he had to step down because of the blind spots that such a style often allows. What we have nurtured in our lives, the things we bring to the table, open doors. Our flaws and faults, if not realized and worked on, will quickly close them.

Balance is about maximizing our strengths while working on our weaknesses so that we do not become self-destructive. The balanced life may not look, at first glance, as spectacular as that of the radical one. Yet Super Achievers are more interested in significance than in showing off.

Life is a marathon, not a sprint. There is no point in rushing to reach the top of the mountain only to finally arrive at the summit so exhausted that one cannot enjoy the view, and having left the important people—family and friends—far below.

The error of externalism is often realized late in life, and by then its consequences may have sabotaged many of the noble plans of youth. Oscar Wilde, whom we quoted at the start of this chapter, was one who too late realized the benefits of balance. He spent the last years of his life in jail on a sodomy charge, and it was then that he probably penned these words:

The gods have given me almost everything, but I let myself be lured into long spells of senseless and sensual ease. Tired of being on the heights, I deliberately went to the depths in search of a new sensation. What paradox was to me in the sphere of thought, perversity became to me in the sphere of passion. I grew careless of the lies of other people. I took pleasure where it pleased me, and passed on. And I forgot that every little action of the common day makes or unmakes character. And that therefore, what one has done in the secret chamber, one has someday to cry aloud from the housetop. I ceased to be lord over myself. I was no longer the captain of my soul, and I did not know it. I allowed pleasure to dominate me, and I ended in horrible disgrace.[35]

FIRST YOU HAVE TO GET OUT OF BED

Discipline

"The alternative to discipline is disaster."

Vance Havner

Chapter Twelve

First You Have to Get out of Bed

The best definition of discipline I have read was given by Scott Peck who wrote that it is *"a process of scheduling the pain and pleasure of life in such a way as to enhance the pleasure by meeting and experiencing the pain first and getting it over with."* First there must be a realization that in life there is both pain and pleasure and that it is impossible to avoid pain. Therefore, the disciplined individual will simply schedule in a way that deals with difficulties and problems quickly so that productivity and pleasure are enhanced.

The disciplined individual deals with problems quickly so that productivity is enhanced.

The businesswoman who has ten things to do today, one of which is to phone an unhappy client, is disciplined if she makes that phone call first. She then feels better about herself and enjoys the rest of the day. However, if she defers the pain to the last thing on the agenda, the foreboding of the call weighs on her throughout the day, thus hindering her effectiveness.

The disciplined parent spends time with the children when they are young, thus building a relationship that will carry them through the possible trauma of teenage years.

Disciplined sports people put time into practice and precision training, knowing that the pain of early mornings and repetitive exercises will be worth it when the games begin.

In a marriage relationship where discipline dictates, problems are dealt with immediately. The command, *"Do not let the sun go down on your wrath"* (Ephesians 4:26 NKJV), if applied, would save many a couple. When bitterness, anger, resentment, and offense are not dealt with in this way, they simply go underground and eventually poison the soil of the relationship.

> Indecisiveness is counterproductive and often creates more pain.

As a husband, it takes discipline, guts, and courage (some would even say stupidity!) to sit down and say to your wife, "Honey, is there anything I do that annoys or frustrates you? I want you to talk with me about it." It takes the same courage for a wife to say this to her husband.

This kind of question launches you into what psychologists would call "the tunnel of chaos"! Vulnerability is difficult, but not to deal with marital problems in an open and honest way simply delays the pain. Discipline realizes that the anguish of honestly dealing with problems now is far less than the pain of separation and divorce later.

Discipline and Decisiveness

The ability to avoid the paralysis of inaction and to defeat the fear of making mistakes is found in the discipline of decisiveness. It takes such discipline to realize that indecision is counterproductive and often creates more pain.

Harry Truman, the United States president between 1945 and 1953, was well known for such decisiveness. This was seen clearly in the decision to drop the atomic bomb on Japan. Historians and political philosophers have argued long and hard, with the benefit of hindsight, over such decisions. Truman made them at the time with both courage and conviction.

Dean Rusk, former secretary of state and close colleague with Truman during his career, spoke highly of this characteristic in the life of the leader:

> *Harry Truman was a genius at making decisions. When he saw a complicated problem, with all the factors in it, it was as though he were looking at a heap of jumbled-up jackstraws. He would listen to all the briefing and think about it. Then he would decide which one of those jackstraws was the crucial one, from his point of view, and he would pull that one out of that complicated pile and make his decision, go home and go to sleep and never look back. He was a genius for that necessary oversimplification at the moment of decision. The alternative of that is paralysis.*[36]

Converting the available information into action is what decision is all about. To know and not to do is not to know at all. The discipline of action, although it may give rise to a mistake, is far preferable to safe and stationary living. Lloyd Jones said, *"The men who try to do something and fail are infinitely better than those who try to do nothing and succeed."*

Developing Discipline

Discipline, I have discovered, has an intrinsic ability to be self-perpetuating.

The individual whose life is totally lacking in discipline need only concentrate on one area of his behavior. It doesn't matter what habit one chooses to reform—diet, exercise, sleeping schedule, or punctuality. For when discipline begins in a corner of one's existence, it will begin to grow, reproduce itself, and breed. A sort of momentum takes over and our disorganized private world, much to our delight and surprise, is quietly conquered.

It is character's version of the domino theory. Yet the process must be started, and much energy expended, in the first month of developing a discipline. Then energy and resolve are produced from this one area—enough to continue and more besides. On the other hand, once there is a break in the pattern, once we allow discouragement, laziness, or even a simple vacation to erode these now well-cemented habits, momentum dies and entropy sets in.

> Discipline is a prerequisite for achievement in life.

Anyone reading this book will probably be of the opinion that discipline is a prerequisite for achievement in life. Yet mere knowledge of one's need for a characteristic does not produce it. What then causes discipline to be developed and practiced in the life of the Super Achiever?

Key to Discipline—A Sense of Destiny

I have already pointed out that having an overriding goal or passion is the key ingredient to success. This is because, once the goal and direction of one's life are set, they produce not only the motivation and the concentration but also the discipline necessary to pay the price for achieving the dream.

Having a vision of where you want to go will create incredible energy to do the hard things necessary to get there. The young man who continually refuses to clean his room, tidy his car, and brush his hair will often do these things without a hassle when the vision of a young lady fills his consciousness.

Vision will also give us strength to persist through the tragedies and injustices of life. The pain of jail, abuse, and unpopularity are more easily tolerated and endured by those who have this sense of destiny.

Indeed, it is often the hard obstacles that test the mettle of our focus, challenge our sense of purpose, and become the making or breaking of our lives.

The strength of our resolve and the power of discipline will come to the forefront in testing times only if our internal direction is well calibrated and our life purpose is nonnegotiable.

Christ said that we must be willing to pick up our cross and follow Him, implying that, in the fulfilling of major dreams, there is pain that must be confronted and lived through. *"If anyone would come after me, he must deny himself and take up his cross and follow me"* (Matthew 16:24 NIV). And many have done this, quite literally following Christ even unto death, motivated by love and purpose not found in this world.

Without this willingness to experience pain for what we believe in, without this discipline, we will not see the vision accomplished. The old weight-lifting maxim rings true here: no pain, no gain. A sense of destiny puts the power of discipline within our grasp.

Enjoy the Price

We have all heard people say, "You've got to pay the price for success," and most of us probably accepted its pragmatism without question. Life experience would declare, however, *"You do not pay the price of success, you enjoy the price of success."* The first time I heard that expression was from the lips of Zig Ziglar. It hit me with real force. You see, we don't pay the price for a successful marriage; we enjoy the price of a successful marriage. We don't pay the price to be fit; we enjoy the price of being fit. We don't pay the price of being good parents; we enjoy the price of being good parents. We don't pay the price for being Super Achievers; we enjoy the price of being Super Achievers. We enjoy seeing our dreams accomplished and our goals reached, resulting in people being helped and our world becoming a better place.

Paradox of Freedom

No man is free who is not master of himself. —Epictetus

In today's world, many do not understand the correlation between discipline and freedom. The truth is that the only really free person is the one who is disciplined.

The athletes who force themselves to train, to put in the long and hard hours, then have the freedom to perform to their potential. The musician who practices is the one who is also able to play from the heart with a freedom and spontaneity that the undisciplined can only watch and admire. The singer who is not willing to learn and practice is not free to sing in the way she desires. The young person who is undisciplined is never free to fulfill the dreams of his heart.

We are most free when we are bound.

We are then most free when we are bound. Scripture proclaims this truth, for it is when we are bound to Christ that we are truly free.

You have been set free from sin and have become slaves to righteousness. I put this in human terms because you are weak in your natural selves. Just as you used to offer the parts of your body in slavery to impurity and to ever-increasing wickedness, so now offer them in slavery to righteousness leading to holiness. When you were slaves to sin, you were free from the control of righteousness. What benefit did you reap at that time from the things you are now ashamed of? Those things result in death! But now that you have been set free from sin and have become slaves to God, the benefit you reap leads to holiness, and the result is eternal life. For the wages of sin is death, but the gift of God is eternal life in Christ Jesus our Lord.

(Romans 6:18–23 NIV)

The Tragedy of Unfulfilled Potential

There is a price for success, but there is an even greater cost in settling for mediocrity and accepting the status quo. More potential has been lost through refusing to pay the price than from any other cause.

The life of Samuel Taylor Coleridge has often been used as an example of how the promise of great talent can be short-circuited by lack of discipline.

> *Coleridge is the supreme tragedy of indiscipline. Never did so great a mind produce so little. He left Cambridge University to join the army; he left the army because he could not rub down a horse; he returned to Oxford and left without a degree. He began a paper called* The Watchman, *which lived for ten numbers and then died. It has been said of him: "He lost himself in visions of work to be done, that always remained to be done. Coleridge had every poetic gift but one—the gift of sustained and concentrated effort." In his hand and in his mind he had all kinds of books, as he said, himself, "Completed save the transcription. I am on the even," he says, "of sending to the press two octavo volumes." But the books were never composed outside Coleridge's mind, because he would not face the discipline of sitting down to write them out. No one ever reached any eminence, and no one having reached it ever maintained it, without discipline.*[37]

The story of Coleridge could be repeated many times through many different people. The difference between the achiever and the Super Achiever often comes down to discipline.

The reason that most die with their music still in them is that they presume upon talent and expect gifting to create success.

This philosophy of life gradually gives rise to a harmful disappointment-driven melancholy, which will eventually permeate every moment of the day.

The loss of discipline will always signal the death of the dream. Enthusiasm and passion have their time. They belong in the race at its beginning and at its end, when the applause of the crowd can be heard. Yet, for the bulk of the race, it is the steady steps, mile after mile, unseen and unappreciated, where discipline is at the forefront.

Without discipline, we have no hope. If our lives fail here, they will cost us everything. But those on the road toward destiny pay the price of discipline with joy. Those who pay it are those who see and understand. The tortoise of such character will always defeat the hare of superficial passion.

I'M BIGGER ON THE INSIDE

Self-Growth

"Our grand business is not to see what lies dimly at a distance, but to do what lies clearly at hand."

Thomas Carlyle

Chapter Thirteen

I'm Bigger on the Inside

I have emphasized that success in life is inside out in nature. Many, however, make the mistake of going to work on what is at a distance, rather than turning their attention to what is close by.

We are not always able to change externals, but internal life changes can be accomplished when we begin to understand this task of personal growth.

The Super Achiever is committed to learn and grow in every area of life.

The Super Achiever is committed to learn and grow in every area of life; to continually push the boundaries, not only in understanding, knowledge, and wisdom, but also in character, attitude, and endurance. This is frequently seen at the most basic level in keeping the body fit, eating right, and exercising so that energy for the day is never a problem. Constant improvement and maintenance of health are outward reflections of this inner value. We must, however, go deeper yet to realize that self-growth is a belief that must pervade and thus affect our whole beings.

Achievers in life are big people or, to use Aristotle's phrase, *"great souled."*

Big people are not simply created by life, genetics, or parental modeling. There has to be the willingness to push the boundaries of one's life, attitude, and heart outward; to move out of the personal comfort zone of nongrowth; and to lead the chase for personal change. It is madness to keep doing the same thing over and over again, expecting different results. We must understand, therefore, that the willingness to think, believe, and act differently is the key to real, visible transformation.

Super Achievers are continually working on their character, emotional responses, and spiritual lives. They realize that success is inside out and that the heart, or the inner core of the person, is where the hardest work must be done. They know that to grow on the outside, you must grow on the inside.

> To grow on the outside, you must grow on the inside.

When, on the other hand, this order is reversed—when there is a sudden expansion of one's external world without a corresponding growth in the internal life—destruction is almost inevitable. The well-documented despair of many who win major prizes through the lottery is a good example of this truth. More money might be in the bank, but often the winners' relational and private worlds are devastated. The internal strength available to them is inadequate to carry and assimilate such an increase in external growth.

For several years, I was involved in teaching children at our local church. I tried to make Children's Church, as we called it, exciting and dynamic. To this end, I would often conduct various chemical experiments, creating explosions and flashes of light. One experiment involved placing a small quantity of water in the bottom of a square gasoline can and heating the can until steam came out of the top. We would then quickly remove the can from the heat, put the lid on tightly, and watch what would happen. Very slowly, the can would begin to crumple until it was squashed and buckled. This happened because a partial vacuum was created within the can and, as it began to cool, the external air pressure eventually crushed the can. The pressure within was far less than the pressure without.

So it is with life. The Super Achiever realizes that personal implosion is a very real possibility unless constant work is carried out on the heart.

Commit yourself to self-growth.

There are many ways of doing this work. Benjamin Franklin practiced a thirteen-week program he created for himself. He wrote down thirteen virtues that he wanted to maintain or practice in his life. These were things such as humility, perseverance, forgiveness, friendliness, and discipline. He then assigned one of these virtues to each week. Throughout each week, he would concentrate on the one assigned virtue, thinking about it and asking questions that brought both analysis and improvement. In this way, by working through the thirteen weeks, he was able to devote at least four weeks of concentrated self-improvement to each of these virtues per year. Later in life, he declared that this practice was probably the key habit of his life that enabled him to achieve everything he did. In simple terms, he was just committing himself, through the use of a practical strategy, to self-growth.

A great benefit of faith in God is that you are continually compelled to be authentic and honest in the evaluation of your weaknesses and faults. Such faith encourages repentance and promises forgiveness. Thus the individual is continually motivated to improve without falling into the ditches of guilt-obsessed, works-based living on the one side or false pride and personal complacency on the other.

Without the decision to grow on the inside, we quickly surrender to marginless living.

Even more comforting is that those who rely on Christ to reform their hearts and lives can count on Him to continue making them better and better until they reach eternity and the perfection of heaven. *"He who began a good work in you will carry it on to completion until the day of Christ Jesus"* (Philippians 1:6 NIV).

Practicing Margin

A personal and practical program of self-growth will not only develop our capabilities in dealing with what life presents to us, but it will also enhance our ability to enjoy it. We will find we have energy left at the end of the day and creativity and ideas left at the end of our problems. If you think about it, it is the only decent way to live.

One author calls this "margin." Without the decision to grow on the inside, we quickly surrender to the continual frustration of marginless living:

Marginless is being thirty minutes late to the doctor's office because you were twenty minutes late getting out of the bank because you were ten minutes late dropping the kids off at school because the car ran out of gas two blocks from the gas station—and you forgot your wallet.

Margin, on the other hand, is having breath left at the top of the staircase, money left at the end of the month, and sanity left at the end of adolescence.[38]

THE UPSIDE OF DOWN

Humility

"The devil did grin for his darling sin is pride that apes humility."

Samuel Taylor Coleridge

Chapter Fourteen

The Upside of Down

John Cleese, well-known for his acting work with Monty Python, has also done more serious work. He was the voice of Screwtape in the audio version of C. S. Lewis's classic book, *The Screwtape Letters*.

Screwtape, a senior devil, writes a series of letters to Wormwood, an apprentice demon, giving advice on how to destroy people's faith. His advice on using humility as a weapon is instructive:

> *Your patient has become humble; have you drawn his attention to the fact? All virtues are less formidable to us once the man is aware that he has them. But this is especially true of humility. Catch him at the moment when he is really poor in spirit and smuggle into his mind the gratifying reflection, "By jove! I'm being humble," and almost immediately pride—pride at his own humility—will appear.[39]*

If only we could all be as perceptive!

The story is told of shipping magnate Mr. Aristotle Onassis, who at the height of his power would conduct board meetings on his luxury yacht. Adjoining his office was a private bathroom and toilet that had been fitted with a one-way mirror on the door, thus enabling Mr. Onassis to take a break from his meeting and yet be able to observe what the participants were doing and saying in his absence.

Mr. Onassis was hosting a business meeting after the ship had been through a major refit, when he felt the call of nature and excused himself. He sat down on the toilet and looked up, expecting to see the meeting continuing. Instead, all he was looking at was a reflection of himself. A workman making minor repairs to the door earlier in the day had replaced the mirror the wrong way around!

Image is everything, so we are rarely honest about our own inadequacies.

We laugh at such stories for several reasons. First, all of us can identify with such experiences. We can all muster a list of personal, embarrassing moments that, despite our attempts to fool the world into thinking we have got it all together, show us up to be what we know we really are— total klutzes. Second, we enjoy hearing about others' mistakes, especially if they are about those who hold positions of prominence or are well-known. Deep down, we suspect that the greats of our world haven't got it together either, and we love the stories that bring out their human sides.

However, we live in a world where having it all together is portrayed as a prerequisite for success. Image is everything, so we are rarely honest about our own inadequacies. Ours is a world of individualism and self-absorption. We have been desensitized to arrogance by the constant call to self-esteem—the call to believe in ourselves and the "I'm-okay, you're-okay" view of humanity. Add to this the basic misunderstanding of what humility really is, and we have the recipe for a world where pride is only thought of in positive terms, a world that also wonders why the sense of serenity and fulfillment does not follow its self-aggrandizement and selfish pursuits.

We need to renew our quest for humility. We need to take this character quality off the scrap heap, where it has been wrongly disposed of. We must take a fresh look at what humility actually is and at the tremendous benefits it brings to those who decide to develop it.

To many, Mohammed Ali, especially in his early years, was arrogance personified. There is a story told, which has not been confirmed, of Ali flying to one of his engagements:

The aircraft ran into foul weather, and mild to moderate turbulence began to toss it about....The passengers were accordingly instructed to fasten their seat belts immediately. Everyone complied but Ali. Noticing this, the flight attendant approached him and requested he follow the captain's order, only to hear Ali audaciously respond, "Superman don't need no seat belt." The flight attendant did not miss a beat and replied, "Superman don't need no airplane either."[40]

What Humility Is Not

Although we often talk about humble circumstances, humility is not based upon externals. Circumstances do not have the ability to make a person humble. There are both humble millionaires and proud prisoners. Sadly, those who are not gifted, whether with talent or material goods, often tend to be the proudest of all. Humility is a condition of the heart, unrelated to position, wealth, or achievement.

Some would define humility as a somewhat pathetic, self-reproving condition, the opposite to self-confidence and a bedfellow of self-pity. The doormat approach to life is an open invitation to those who abuse, use, and manipulate. Such an attitude in life will do nothing to build self-respect or mature relationships.

We may desire to call this humility, but to do so is to malign a God-given quality. True humility increases the individual's effectiveness and serenity, while this impostor—this wolf in sheep's clothing, this cowardly self-deprecation—never develops, only destroys.

> True humility is always a sign of inner strength.

Humility has received much bad press due to these pale imitators.

We must come to realize that true humility is always a sign of inner strength and never a symptom of weakness or self-doubt.

Humility Defined

Humility is the internal quality that prefers others and exalts them while appraising one's self realistically. It is not so much a putting down of one's self as much as it is the lifting up of others.

Humility realizes that the only decent way to live is to be motivated beyond yourself; to serve and help others, to be more interested in the giving than the getting. When this principle becomes an inner value and is practiced with consistency, the getting will take care of itself. Zig Ziglar has put it this way: *"You can have everything in life that you want if you will just help enough other people get what they want."*

Why Be Humble?

Number One—The Mysteries of Life

The story is told of how President Theodore Roosevelt and his friend, naturalist William Beebe, would often go outside after dining together and look up at the stars. They would first look for a patch of light in the night sky near Pegasus, and then they would both say together the following few sentences: *"That is the spiral galaxy in Andromeda. It is as large as our Milky Way. It is one of a hundred million galaxies. It consists of one hundred billion suns, each larger than our own."*

They would turn to one another and say, *"Now I think we are small enough! Let's go to bed."* Then they would retire for the evening.

I personally believe that the latest scientific discoveries from the world of quantum mechanics and astrophysics heighten this awareness. It seems the more we learn about the origin of the universe and the processes of life, the more we are amazed.

The entire cosmos, it seems, is balancing on a series of razor blades—finely tuned characteristics, each necessary for life to be possible. This phenomenon is known as the anthropic principle. As the months go by and our knowledge increases, so this principle rapidly becomes more and more impressive.

Cosmologist Edward Harrison states,

Here is the cosmological proof of the existence of God—the design argument of Paley—updated and refurbished. The fine-tuning of the universe provides prima facie evidence of deistic design. Take your choice: blind chance that requires multitudes of universes or design that requires only one....Many scientists, when they admit their views, incline toward the teleological or design argument.[41]

Hugh Ross, in his book *The Creator and the Cosmos*, lists 25 such characteristics for the universe and a further 32 for our planet. The razor-blade analogy is, if anything, too generous. Take, for example, one parameter that has to do with the electromagnetic force relative to gravity. If this was increased by one part in 10^{40} (that's 10 with 40 zeros after it!), only small stars would form. If it was decreased by just one part in 10^{40}, only large stars would form.

The entire cosmos is balancing on a series of razor blades.

For life to be possible in the universe, both large and small stars must exist. The former produce life's essential elements (everything from cobalt to thallium), and the latter are the only stars that are stable enough and burn long enough to sustain a planet with life.

The narrowness of this parameter cannot be overemphasized. Ross gives the example of marking a nickel with a red cross and then throwing it into a pile of unmarked nickels—a pile so large it covers the whole of Australia up to the height of the moon. Now multiply this pile by one trillion. The chance that a blindfolded man would pick the red nickel on his first attempt is one in 10^{40}![3]

Remember, this is just one of the razor blades.

Tony Rothman, a theoretical physicist in an essay on this anthropic principle said,

> *When confronted with the order and beauty of the universe and the strange coincidences of nature, it's very tempting to take a leap of faith from science into religion. I am sure many physicists want to. I only wish they would admit it.*[43]

More and more physicists are admitting it. Robert Griffiths, who won the Heinemann prize in mathematical physics, observed, *"If we need an atheist for a debate, we go to the philosophy department. The physics department isn't much use."*

> Humility is enhanced the more we grow and the more we learn.

This, then, is why humility is enhanced the more we grow and the more we learn.

We will continue to learn, to explore, to stretch beyond ourselves. This is one attribute that makes us truly human— the search for truth. The more we discover of the puzzle, the more impressed we are with its Manufacturer.

This fascination with the universe around us and the desire to learn is also accompanied by something far deeper.

There comes a time, I believe, in the existence of every human being when we suddenly realize the enormity and wonder of creation and the seeming insignificance of our own lives. Couple this with the inner awareness of a Creator—a Creator who deems us highly significant, indeed the crowning accomplishment of His creation—and we are filled with a real sense of humble reverence and awe. Isn't this awe of God and His holiness, combined with His endless love for us, the reason for the teaching and practice of worship?

Worship enables us to maintain a healthy perspective on who we are and who God is. The fanciful doctrines of the New Age movement, in which all of us are actually gods ourselves, know nothing of this. Pantheism offers a short-term sense of being in control, where self is worshipped, but in the final analysis self fails to perform as the god of all feeling and meaning. Practicing the worship of God in our existence, thoughts, and actions is a major key in allowing the characteristic of humility to develop within us.

Number Two—The Dark Side

Out of the crooked timber of humanity, no straight thing was ever made.　　　　　　　—Immanuel Kant

Humility recognizes that all of us are created and engineered for success and achievement, and yet, at the same time, knows that within us all there is a dark side. But most of us don't want to come to terms with that. The, "I'm-okay, you're-okay," philosophy of life, it turns out, is not the only thought system confusing the reality of our innate sinfulness. The blame mentality is also responsible, as it has exacerbated the false sense of our own uprightness.

This refusal to take personal responsibility, the redefinition of sin as sickness, and the reduction of punishment to merely rehabilitation have all contributed to our sense of cosmic smugness.

The truth is, we are incapable of being totally pure and right in our thoughts, motives, and actions. Without calling on divine help, we are incapable of rising above the misery of the human condition.

Without divine help, we are incapable of rising above the misery of the human condition.

This dark side is not just exhibited in the evil despots who have come and gone, but also in the phenomena of group evil. Group evil occurs when normal men and women stand by and allow that which is wrong to prevail, perhaps because speaking out would cause personal harm or loss of popularity. Deep down, we all know that if the secrets of our hearts were laid bare, we would not be proud of our records.

The *Times of London* once produced an article entitled, "What's Wrong with the World?" G. K. Chesterton, the English writer, replied, *"I am. Yours truly, G. K. Chesterton."*

Number Three—Diversity of People

Pride is often the result of overvaluing one's own talents or undervaluing those of others. Humility, however, is not into comparisons. Although I may have certain strengths, abilities, or skills that others do not, I also have weaknesses, flaws, and faults that others do not share. In short, if my humility, or for that matter, my pride, is based upon what I can or cannot do, I am deluded.

True humility recognizes that we are all wired differently. We all have, in the words of the New Testament, *"different gifts"* (Romans 12:6 NIV). We maintain our balance and perspective when we think of ourselves in this light. We all have, as it were, something we can offer and bring to the table.

It is our obligation to use what God has given us for the common good and for His glory. Humble people understand this and use their gifts confidently. When praise comes, they do not take the adulation to heart; instead, they thank their Creator for making them so.

Continuing the Quest

The wonders of creation, our inability to obtain perfection, and the variety of gifts and abilities given to different people all beckon to us to embrace humility. In fact, they show fairly conclusively the foolishness of pride. Yet pride comes so easily to us while attaining humility seems to be an impossible task. The quest for humility is a hard one, but rewarding. Scripture says that God will exalt the humble.

All of you, clothe yourselves with humility toward one another, because, "God opposes the proud but gives grace to the humble." Humble yourselves, therefore, under God's mighty hand, that he may lift you up in due time.

(1 Peter 5:5–6 NIV)

FORTUNE FAVORS THE BRAVE

Courage

"All our dreams can come true if we have the courage to pursue them."

Walt Disney

Chapter Fifteen

Fortune Favors the Brave

There is something about courage that is incredibly inspiring. Whether one sees it in real life or reads about it in history, courage never fails to grab the heart and motivate the soul.

Hollywood has been quick to recognize this, and so it tends to be the only secret of a Super Achiever we find regularly on our screens. Courage is portrayed as Rocky Balboa takes on a superior opponent or Arnold Schwarzenegger faces an all-powerful class of kindergarten children. Butch Cassidy and the Sundance Kid had it, and so did the Karate Kid. Call me a barbarian, call me culturally impaired, but I enjoyed these films. I may not get an invitation to Cannes with such an admission, but there is something about raw courage and primitive man going against the elements that gets the testosterone flowing.

Courage, of course, knows no gender boundaries. It is just that most men only recognize and appreciate it when it is conveyed in digital sound, wide-screen, macho-type films. Yet deep down, most of us guys realize that if a Bond or a Rambo had to contemplate the experience of childbirth, their carefully crafted façades would crumble at the first contraction!

Courage comes in many different forms, but when it comes to us we must grab it, because success in life desperately needs its strength.

One cannot read a book like *Reach for the Sky*, view a film such as *Schindler's List*, or listen to a war-time speech by Churchill without sensing the courage rising. When we have courage, we can face the future with confidence. Courage enables us to endure our present problems with a tenacity that never gives in. Courage makes us stronger, braver, and better people.

Courage is not the absence of fear; it is the ability to face fear.

Merriam-Webster's 11th Collegiate Dictionary defines courage as, *"mental or moral strength to venture, persevere, and withstand danger, fear, or difficulty."*

Courage is not the absence of fear; it is the ability to face fear and say, "Regardless of how I feel at the moment, I am going to push through to the other side."

Courage realizes that fear, more often than not, is illogical. Allowing fear to dominate makes the problem worse. Michel de Montaigne said, *"He who fears he will suffer, already suffers because of his fear."*

Churchill, whose life epitomized this virtue, had this to say:

> One ought never to turn one's back on a threatened danger and try to run away from it. If you do that, you will double the danger. But if you meet it promptly and without flinching, you will reduce the danger by half. Never run away from anything. Never!

Those who achieve success realize that life involves some element of risk. One cannot cover every base. Success is never guaranteed. Ineffectiveness comes on the wings of fear. When the "what if's" loom larger in our consciousness than the "why not's," then cowardice rules over courage and dreams go unfulfilled.

Pioneering always takes courage. As the Spanish poet Antonio Machado put it, *"Traveler, there is no path. Paths are made by walking."* Courage ventures from the path and leads the way. It dares to be different and, as a result, expands the circle of human experience.

The bears, lions, and Goliaths of life will never retreat of their own accord. They must be faced.

Fear says run. Courage stops and fights.

Our culture must fight for what is right and good; this fight becomes impossible when the will has gone or the nerve to stand up for truth has faltered.

> **Fear says run. Courage stops and fights.**

The life experiences of Solzhenitsyn caused him to write and warn of bravery's demise: *"Must one point out that from ancient times a decline in courage has been considered the beginning of the end?"*

Jesus' courage was seen in His willingness to die on the cross for our sins. He had many opportunities to change His mind and deny that He was God, thus saving His life. He could have done it when the high priest, Caiaphas, asked Him whether or not He was the Messiah, but He didn't. He could have told Pilate that He was not the King of the Jews when Pilate asked. Jesus could have chosen to speak to Herod and plead for His life, but instead He remained silent and went forward to the purpose He had come to carry out.

Daniel facing Goliath, Churchill facing Hitler, Lincoln facing his self-doubt, Joan of Arc facing the fire—all who achieve rely heavily on courage.

This virtue has been the key to many of the world's Super Achievers.

Courage is the by-product of faith and the child of destiny.

Jack Lemmon has said he tries to harness his fears and use them to work for him: *"Failure seldom stops you. What stops you is the fear of failure."*

Others showed their courage, like Mary Kay, who invested all her retirement money into her new, risky business. Kris Kristofferson left his secure career in the army to pursue the untested and unknown future of songwriting. When asked what qualities had helped him the most, he replied, *"A creative imagination and a compassion for my fellows and strength of spirit, which doesn't come from me but from God. I think I have a strong spirit. I allow my spirit to be strong."*

Courage itself very rarely stands alone. It is the by-product of faith and the child of destiny. This is, of course, one of the greatest discoveries of the Super Achiever: that a characteristic such as purpose, once cultivated, produces naturally the necessary ingredients to fulfill itself.

This is true of most virtues. With humor comes perspective and with perspective, peace. Focus produces both clarity and energy, while humility enables us to believe in others and continue to grow in knowledge and wisdom.

When the decision is made, and the journey is embarked upon with conviction, the soul finds much help along the way.

Conversely, negative habits, attitudes, and character traits compound, working against the individual and his success: Pride results in a loss of information and relationships; unforgiveness destroys our life perspectives and causes us to lose focus; hope and humor are not nurtured when we allow despondency to dog our paths or apathy to paralyze our progress.

The domino effect will work either to our advantage or disadvantage. The heart, as it were, looks after those who look after it. The old dictum rings true—God helps those who help themselves!

The neglect of our inner world will slowly suck meaning out of our existence. Like quicksand, the melancholy of emptiness will finally have its inevitable victory.

Perhaps this is why the imperative of Proverbs must be heeded: *"Above all else, guard your heart, for it is the wellspring of life"* (Proverbs 4:23 NIV).

EPILOGUE
Further on, Further in

"In actual life, every great enterprise begins with and takes its first forward step in faith."

Friedrich Schlegel

Epilogue

Our journey together has discovered and explored some qualities I believe are essential for success in life.

Obviously, this particular study on *Secrets of Super Achievers* is not exhaustive, yet its lessons are compelling:

- The health of the soul, inside-out living, and ordering and expanding the inner world are the keys to finding ourselves and reaching our potential.

- The problem and the answer both lie within our hearts, and therefore within our reach.

- The journey outward is not nearly as important or fruitful as the journey inward; our spiritual lives must be nurtured if we are going to be the people we dream of.

It seems strange that, despite these truths, which I believe are self-evident and resonate within us all, our society and our culture continue in the worship of dead and impotent gods—selfishness and escapism, non-responsibility, and accumulation. We are born for better things than these. Deep down, we know the truth, but for some reason we don't live it out.

That "better thing" we are born for is a true relationship with God. But we can't always quite get there because each of us has a natural inclination toward sin—sin that our perfect God hates and that leads to death. We love sin; we can't help ourselves. But God can help us. He sent His Son Jesus to earth to die for our sins so that we could be restored to our right relationship with Him—so that we could be His children again. All that remains for us to do is accept the gift of salvation He has extended to us; to say, "God, I know I am sinful and helpless without You. Thank You for sending Your Son to die on the cross so that my sin would be paid for, not by my death, but by Jesus' perfect sacrifice. I accept His sacrifice for my sins, and I want God to be the Guide and Ruler of my life."

A Chosen Life

"Whatever will be, will be," is wrong!

Great lives are not stumbled upon—they require desire, determination, and faith. They don't just happen by chance—they are chosen! Chosen by those who get desperate enough to buck the system and say, "No," to the security of mediocrity. Chosen by those who rouse themselves from the slumber of complacency and self-depreciation.

There is, you see, a strange malady sweeping our land—one akin to sleeping sickness or chronic fatigue syndrome. This ailment does not, however, strike the body but the heart. Truth, which generations before us have felt no hesitation in dying for, now draws only a slight smile and nod of passive agreement from us. The passion has been absorbed by the pleasure, the fire has gone out of our faith. The stakes are still sky-high, but for us it doesn't seem to matter any more.

Our lives, contrary to popular belief, are not some kind of Hollywood blockbuster, where danger threatens us as we watch, munching our popcorn and knowing it's all just pretend.

The forces arrayed against us are real. Eternity flows ahead of us. If we sleep now, we do so at our own peril.

Let us take courage. Stand and fight. Let us be who we are meant to be. Life is for living. The years are passing. The time for decision is now!

Endnotes

1   George Gilder, *Wealth and Poverty* (New York: Basic Books, Inc., Publishers, 1981).

2   Malcolm Muggeridge, *Chronicles of Wasted Time: The Green Stick* (New York: William Morrow & Company, Inc., 1973).

3   Herbert Butterfield, *Christianity and History* (New York: Charles Scribner's Sons, 1950).

4   John C. Maxwell, *Developing the Leader within You* (Nashville: Thomas Nelson, Inc., 1993).

5   Ibid.

6   Samuel S. Marquis, *Henry Ford: An Interpretation* (Boston: Little, Brown & Co., 1923).

7   David Myers, *The Pursuit of Happiness* (New York: Avon Books, 1993).

8   Ogden Nash, "Don't Grin or You'll Have to Bear It," *I'm a Stranger Here Myself* (Boston: Little, Brown & Co., 1938).

9   Unknown author, as quoted by Glen Schultz, *Kingdom Education: God's Plan for Educating Future Generations* (Nashville: Lifeway Press 1998).

10   George Gilder, *Wealth and Poverty* (New York: Basic Books, Inc., Publishers, 1981).

11   Vaclav Havel, *Disturbing the Peace* (New York: Vintage, 1991).

12   Viktor E. Frankl, *Man's Search for Meaning*, revised and updated (New York: Washington Square Press, 1984).

13   B. Eugene Greissman, *The Achievement Factors: Candid Interviews with Some of the Most Successful People of Our Time* (New York: Dodd, Mead, and Company, 1987).

14 William J. Hinson, as quoted by John Maxwell, *Developing the Leader Within You* (Nashville: Thomas Nelson, Inc., 1993).

15 William Shakespeare, *Hamlet*, Act III, scene i.

16 Dr. Chris Thurman, *The Truths We Must Believe* (Nashville: Thomas Nelson, Inc., 1991).

17 Ravi Zacharias, *Can Man Live Without God?* (Nashville: W Publishing Group, 1994).

18 B. Eugene Greissman, *The Achievement Factors: Candid Interviews with Some of the Most Successful People of Our Time* (New York: Dodd, Mead, and Company, 1987).

19 Dr. F. Carlton Booth, as quoted by Ted W. Engstrom, *The Pursuit of Excellence* (Grand Rapids: Zondervan, 1982).

20 Paul Zane Pilzer, *God Wants You to Be Rich* (New York: Fireside, 1995).

21 Ibid.

22 Ibid.

23 George Gilder, *Wealth and Poverty* (New York: Basic Books, Inc., Publishers, 1981).

24 G. K. Chesterton, "The Twelve Men," *Tremendous Trifles* (New York: Dodd, Mead, & Co., 1909).

25 Robert Jones, "Punch Lines," *Inprint* (1991), 73.

26 Ravi Zacharias, *Can Man Live Without God?* (Nashville: W Publishing Group, 1994).

27 From Alister E. McGrath, *Intellectuals Don't Need God and Other Modern Myths* (Grand Rapids: Zondervan, 1993), paraphrased by Ravi Zacharias, *Can Man Live Without God?* (Nashville: W Publishing Group, 1994).

28 David G. Myers, *The Pursuit of Happiness* (New York: Avon Books, 1993).

29   Ibid.

30   Ibid.

31   Margery Williams, *The Velveteen Rabbit* (New York: Doubleday and Company, Inc., 1958), as quoted by Swindoll, *Improving Your Serve* (Nashville: W Publishing Group, 1981).

32   Blaise Pascal, *Thoughts*.

33   Richard A. Swenson, *Margin* (Colorado Springs: NavPress, 1992).

34   Ibid.

35   Steve Farrar, *Finishing Strong* (Sisters, Oregon: Multnomah Publishers, Inc., 1995).

36   B. Eugene Greissman, *The Achievement Factors: Candid Interviews with Some of the Most Successful People of Our Time* (New York: Dodd, Mead, and Company, 1987).

37   William Barclay, *The Letters to the Galatians and Ephesians* (Philadelphia: Westminster, 1976), as quoted by Gordon McDonald, *Ordering Your Private World* (Nashville: Thomas Nelson, Inc., 2003).

38   Dr. Richard A. Swenson, *Margin* (Colorado Springs: NavPress, 2004).

39   C. S. Lewis, *Screwtape Letters*, performed by John Cleese (n.p.: Audio Literature, 1999).

40   As told by Ravi Zacharias, *Can Man Live Without God?* (Nashville: W Publishing Group, 1994).

41   Edward Harrison, as quoted by Hugh Ross, *The Creator and the Cosmos: How the Latest Scientific Discoveries of the Century Reveal God* (Colorado Springs: NavPress, 2001).

42   Ibid.

43   Ibid.

About the Author

An international speaker and best-selling author, Philip Baker began speaking publicly at the young age of nineteen and since that time has appeared before businesspeople, conferences, and churches in most countries around the world, with audiences ranging from fifty people to ten thousand. Philip is both a brilliant communicator, who knows his subject, and a great entertainer, with the ability to combine solid content with humor.

Philip is the senior pastor of Riverview Church, one of Australia's largest churches. He continually works to develop unity with other churches and ministers, which has helped to build a strong Christian network both in Australia and throughout the world.

Philip lives in Perth, Australia, with his wife, Heather. They have three daughters.

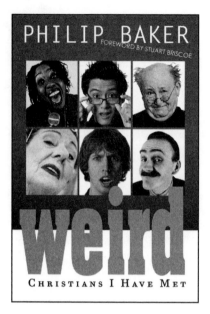

Weird Christians I Have Met
Philip Baker

Best-selling author Phil Baker takes a lighthearted approach in his plea for balance in the Christian life. His refreshing look at Christian character is the result of both observation and experience and includes such fascinating characters as End-Time Ed, Judgmental Jill, and Pentecostal Pamela. And Phil isn't just pointing fingers. "I could have called this book Weird Christians I Have Been," he says, "because several of them seem strangely familiar to me."
We are all on a journey and can easily wander off the road, spinning our tires on the gravelly shoulder. Let Phil help you get back on track and on the road to true Christlike character.

ISBN: 0-88368-805-0 • Trade • 144 pages

www.whitakerhouse.com

www.deepercalling.com

Power Points for Success
Bob Harrison

Let one of America's most effective motivational speakers help you improve or completely transform your life—one step at a time. In his signature enthusiastic style, Bob Harrison guides you through a variety of life's challenges, revealing how you can be an overcomer and experience increase in every area of your life. Bob's principles of increase show how to change your mind-set and build yourself up so that you can live a victorious life—physically, mentally, financially, spiritually, and relationally. Through his success strategies, Bob has positively impacted homes, businesses, and organizations around the nation and world. With *Power Points,* you can benefit from these same strategies. As you activate the truths in this book—presented in a practical and easy-to-understand manner—your life can take on dramatic new direction and power.

ISBN: 0-88368-406-3 • Hardcover • 240 pages

www.whitakerhouse.com

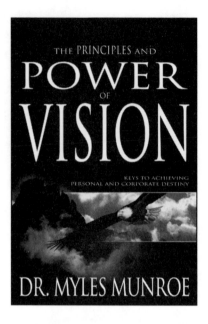

The Principles and Power of Vision
Dr. Myles Munroe

Whether you are a businessperson, a homemaker, a student, or a head of state, best-selling author Dr. Myles Munroe explains how you can make your dreams and hopes a living reality. Your success is not dependent on the state of the economy or what the job market is like. You do not need to be hindered by the limited perceptions of others or by a lack of resources. Discover time-tested principles that will enable you to fulfill your vision no matter who you are or where you come from.

You were not meant for a mundane or mediocre life. Revive your passion for living, pursue your dream, discover your vision—and find your true life.

ISBN: 0-88368-951-0 • Hardcover • 240 pages

WHITAKER
HOUSE

www.whitakerhouse.com

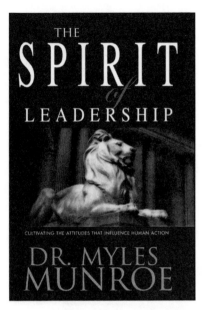

The Spirit of Leadership
Dr. Myles Munroe

Leaders may be found in boardrooms, but they may also be found in families, schools, and organizations of all kinds—anywhere people interact, nurture, create, or build. Contrary to popular opinion, leadership is not meant for an elite group of people who—by fate or accident—are allowed to be leaders while everyone else is consigned to being lifelong followers. After personally training thousands of leaders from around the world, best-selling author Dr. Myles Munroe reports that while all people possess leadership potential, many do not understand how to cultivate the leadership nature and how to apply it to their lives. Discover the unique attitudes that all effective leaders exhibit, how to eliminate hindrances to your leadership abilities, and how to fulfill your particular calling in life. With wisdom and power, Dr. Munroe reveals a wealth of practical insights that will move you from being a follower to becoming the leader you were meant to be!

ISBN: 0-88368-983-9 • Hardcover • 304 pages

www.whitakerhouse.com

You the Leader
Phil Pringle

Do you envision future possibilities that others don't? Are you a "can-do" person? Do creative solutions to the challenges of life stir in your heart and soul? Or, have you buried these leadership characteristics deep inside because you have bought the lie that you are just a follower, not a leader? The truth is that this world is in desperate need of good, godly leaders—in other words, you and your God-given abilities. Drawing from Scripture, personal experience, and the writings of both contemporary and historical leaders, pastor Phil Pringle offers practical insights into effective leadership that can be applied in every arena of life, not just inside church walls. As you examine the attributes of dynamic leaders and the kingdom principles that govern their lives, you will discover how to realize your personal leadership potential. Explore how to implement the vision God has instilled in you—and enjoy the process of becoming the leader He has called you to be!

ISBN: 0-88368-814-X • Hardcover • 320 pages

WHITAKER
HOUSE

www.whitakerhouse.com